# The Mindful Menopause Workbook

# The Mindful Menopause Workbook

## Workbook   DAILY PRACTICES

Francesca Dupraz-Brossard

Wisdom Publications
199 Elm Street
Somerville, MA 02144 USA
wisdomexperience.org

*Library of Congress Cataloging-in-Publication Data*
Names: Dupraz-Brossard, Francesca, author.
Title: The mindful menopause workbook: daily practices /
    Francesca Dupraz-Brossard.
Description: First Wisdom edition. | Somerville: Wisdom Publications, [2021] |
    Includes bibliographical references.
Identifiers: LCCN 2021024469 (print) | LCCN 2021024470 (ebook) |
    ISBN 9781614296492 (paperback) | ISBN 9781614296508 (ebook)
Subjects: LCSH: Menopause—Popular works. | Menopause—Psychological aspects.
Classification: LCC RG186 .D88 2021 (print) | LCC RG186 (ebook) |
    DDC 618.1/75—dc23
LC record available at https://lccn.loc.gov/2021024469
LC ebook record available at https://lccn.loc.gov/2021024470

ISBN 978-1-61429-649-2    ebook ISBN 978-1-61429-650-8

25 24 23 22 21
5 4 3 2 1

Cover photo by Mona Eendra. Cover design by Phil Pascuzzo. Interior design by Gopa & Ted 2, Inc.

Printed on acid-free paper that meets the guidelines for permanence and durability of the
Production Guidelines for Book Longevity of the Council on Library Resources.

Printed in the United States of America.

I dedicate the journal to my three daughters, Zain, Sara, and Tala, who have supported me with their humor throughout this journey that unfolded from the journeys before. They have made me aware of life's precious stages, and I hope that one day they will be able to use the resources in the book.

# Contents

Introduction                                                                1

**JOURNAL**
Daily Practices: January–December                                           5

**MEDITATIONS**                                                           405
  Positions for Meditation                                       405
  Common Obstacles and Challenges to Meditation                  407
  The Raisin Exercise                                            407
  Abdominal Breathing                                            408
  Three-Minute Breathing Space                                   409
  Five-Minute Mindful Breathing Meditation                       409
  Five-Minute Self-Compassion Break                              410
  Walk the Mindfulness Walk—Ten-Minute Walking Meditation        410
  Metta (Loving-Kindness) Meditation                             411
  Body-Scan Meditation                                           411
  Guided Meditation to Get to Sleep                              412

**YOGA**                                                                  415
STANDING POSES                                                            418
  Mountain Pose (*Tadasana*)                                     418
  Neck Rolls (*Kantasanchalasana*)                              419
  Side Bend in Mountain Pose (*Parshva Tadasana*)               419
  Shoulder Shrugs                                                420
  Torso Twists in Mountain Pose (*Parivritta Tadasana*)          420

Palm Tree Pose (*Talasana*)     421

Upward Salute (*Urdhva Hastasana*)     422

Five-Pointed Star (*Utthita Tadasana*)     422

Extended Triangle Pose (*Utthita Trikonasana*)     422

Tree Pose (*Vrikshasana*)     423

Eagle Pose (*Garudasana*)     424

Equestrian/Low-Lunge Pose (*Ashva Sanchalanasanaa*)     424

Warrior Pose I (*Virabhadrasana I*)     425

Warrior Pose II (*Virabhadrasana II*)     426

Warrior Pose III (*Virabhadrasana III*)     427

Standing Forward Bend (*Uttanasana*)     427

Revolved Wide-Legged Forward Fold (*Parivritta Prasarita Padottanasana*)     428

SITTING POSES     429

Staff Pose (*Dandasana*)     429

Revolved Head-to-Knee Pose (*Parivritta Janu Shirshasana*)     429

Cow-Face Pose (*Gomukhasana*)     430

Half Spinal Twist (*Ardha Matsyendrasana*)     431

Cobbler's Pose/Bound-Angle Pose (*Baddha Konasana*)     431

Head to Knee Pose (*Janu Shirshasana*)     432

Lion Pose (*Simhasana*)     433

PRONE POSES     433

Downward-Facing Dog Pose (*Adho Mukha Shvanasana*)     433

Plank Pose (*Phalakasana*)     434

Cat-Cow Pose (*Bidilasana-Marjaryasana*)     435

Sunbird Pose (*Dandayamana Bharmanasana*)     436

BACKBENDS     436

Cobra Pose (*Bhujangasana*)     436

Upward-Facing Dog Pose (*Urdhva Mukha Shvanasana*)     437

King Cobra Pose (*Raja Bhujangasana*)     437

Half-Locust Pose (*Ardha Shalabhasana*)     438

Locust Pose (*Shalabhasana*)     439

Bridge Pose (*Setu Bandha Sarvangasana*)     439

Fish Pose (*Matsyasana*)     440

Camel Pose (*Ushtrasana*)     441

SUPINE POSES     442

Wind-Relief Pose/Knee-to-Chest Pose (*Apanasana*)     442

Reclined Spinal Twist (*Supta Matsyendrasana*)     442

Straight-Leg Raise (*Eka Pada Uttana Padasana*)     443

Side-Reclining Vishnu Couch Pose (*Anantasana*)     444

INVERSIONS     445

Plow Pose (*Halasana*)     445

Headstand (*Shirshasana*)     445

RESTORATIVE POSES     446

Half-Inverted Pose, Legs Up a Wall (*Viparita Karani*)     446

Wide-Knee Child's Pose (*Utthita Balasana*)     447

Child's Pose (*Balasana*)     447

Reverse Corpse Pose (*Advasana*)     448

Corpse Pose (*Shavasana*)     448

Shopping List     451

References     453

About the Author     457

# Introduction

WELCOME TO YOUR mindful menopause workbook! This space has been lovingly created for women entering or going through menopause, whether naturally or after surgery. As the lifespan of women has extended, we can expect to spend thirty to forty years post-menopause. My contemporaries expect and hope to be healthy, attractive, productive, and happy throughout their lives, yet menopause can make this difficult as libido drops and physical energy and memory decline. Pain and illness can increase, and bone density and muscle-mass reduction can begin to compromise physical strength. Mood swings and sleepiness can rob women of their sense of balance. Upon reflection, I realized that many of these issues plague younger women during their menstrual cycle too. We women are governed by our hormones!

I created this mindfulness workbook to be an enjoyable source of self-inquiry, reflection, growth, and discovery throughout the year during a period in the life cycle that is often a challenge for women. Research in mindfulness has burgeoned, and the results are being published in peer-reviewed journals. Mindfulness is more than a technique that has been well integrated into mainstream medicine, psychotherapy, and popular culture. It is a way of being that can be continually honed with time and practice. Mindfulness practice is growing in success and expanding its application to different areas. It has its origins in Buddhist philosophy but is secular. People of any religious denomination, or none, can practice it. Mindfulness is really quite simple. According to one of its founding Western proponents, Jon Kabat-Zinn, it is the act of "paying attention on purpose, in the present moment, and non-judgmentally."*

The menopausal-related issues to be touched upon in this journal mindfully will be:

- ✦ Mood issues
- ✦ Weight gain
- ✦ Fatigue
- ✦ Sleep
- ✦ Hot flashes
- ✦ Sexuality

*Kabat-Zinn, *Wherever You Go, There You Are*, 4.

Obviously, this list is by no means exhaustive. To keep the practice to a minimal and realistic investment (although you are free to go further), I have had to be succinct!

As mindfulness has already been found to help treat separate problems that are all common to menopause, mindfulness is also able to help women relieve menopausal symptoms. The workbook format and journaling, though not allowing the same benefits as participating in eight-week mindfulness programs, has certain advantages—it is a playful activity that can be performed at your own time and place. This workbook allows women to get a taste, and some of the advantages, of longer, more specialized programs. In the future, forums and retreats might ensue for women from the workbook and diary format.

I invite you to use this workbook every day, even if you only have enough time to read the entry of the day and take a few moments to become aware of your experience, draw a deep breath, and close your eyes. You will need to set aside some time and be committed. Obviously, the more you can engage with the material and exercises, the more benefit you will derive. If you miss a day, or more, you can catch up later. The best time to check in would be when you wake up. This will give you plenty of time to think about the exercise beforehand and then come back at the end of the day before you go to sleep. There is space on every page where you can jot down your moment-to-moment awareness of thoughts, emotions, and bodily sensations in response to the instructions and exercises or simply as your day and awareness unfold naturally. A small icon comes before the meditation exercises ◯ and the yoga poses ✳.

The aim of the daily entries is micro self-care and self-development mentally, physically, and spiritually, following the mindfulness tradition. I hope these small daily seeds will germinate over time. The latest scientific research shows that the brain is capable of neuroplasticity. Neuroplasticity is helped along if one reinforces the positive changes one wants with brief, repetitive experiences. We know that physical health depends too on proper nutrition, exercise, and rest. You can combine the daily exercises and practices with macro self-care practices (sports, beauty treatments, religious practices, cultural activities, socializing, etc.) according to your time, energy, and motivation.

This workbook has a section on hatha yoga asanas (poses). The asanas and sequences will help ease the most common issues facing women at menopause, such as low energy, poor sleep, and anxiety. Feel free to create your own sequences as well. Let them inspire you to reacquaint yourself with your strengths and limitations and experience the joy of gradually progressing in your mental and physical flexibility at your own pace. There are also meditations for specific practices and menopause-related issues.

The book in no way purports to replace medical advice or care from your general practitioner, gynecologist, or psychotherapist. Please listen to and be aware of your individual needs. The important thing is to learn, grow, and have fun!

This workbook evolved from the final project of an Advanced Certificate in Mindfulness-Based Interventions (MBI) at the University of Geneva and The Haute École de Santé Suisse in Geneva, Switzerland, from 2017 to 2018. At the same time, I completed a 500-hour European Alliance yoga teacher training course in Switzerland in Kundalini yoga. I am completing my mindfulness teacher training with the Oxford Mindfulness Centre. I wish to thank all my teachers, supervisors, colleagues, and patients, who teach me so much at every moment.

I would like to thank my loving husband, Olivier, who is always curious, respectful, and open to discussing women's topics. Thank you to Lionel Fouassier for the photography of the yoga poses and to his sister Sara for her artistic advice during the photo shoot. Finally, I want to give a heartfelt thank you to Wisdom Publications for believing in me. We all need to have the faith of others to give us hope, and with hope almost anything is possible.

The photos (except those of the yoga postures) are my own, taken throughout my mindfulness journey in 2017–18. Many depict changing landscapes in Switzerland, a country where the four seasons remind one of the rhythms of life, which we become more aware of in menopause. During the mindfulness retreat as part of the MBI course, I experienced a surge of creativity hitherto in reserve and unexplored, and I began writing poetry. Unless otherwise stated, the poems included here are the fruits of this newfound inspiration. Mindfulness has helped me sail the journey of menopause with serenity and ample resources. May you too have many self-discoveries, as well as peace and happiness, throughout your own journey.

With my warmest regards,
Francesca Dupraz-Brossard

# Journal

# January

Snow on my skin,
alpine awakening,
mountain air in my alveoli,
invigorate my memory.
Hovering in quiet reverie,
the gossamer mist draping,
by the golden eagle gravitating.
January's here, a brand new year!
The dash of daunted deer,
a new month refreshing,
alive to each beginning.

## 1

We start the year full of great resolutions that often don't last until the end of January. In fact, according to statistics only 8 percent of people stick to their resolutions.* Instead of resolutions, what about trying intentions? Find the personal meaning in making changes, focusing on the process rather than the results. For example, how about swapping the resolution to lose weight with the intention to go for walks in nature and eat wholesome foods? Chances are you will lose some weight and enjoy the journey. What unhelpful habits support the behaviors you wish to change?

The word "resolution" stems from the Latin *resolvere*—to reduce into simpler forms. That's what I would like you to do regarding your resolutions. Bring awareness to your behavior. For example, when, why, and where do you overeat, or eat the wrong foods?

_____

_____

_____

_____

_____

_____

_____

_____

_____

_____

_____

_____

_____

_____

*"New Year's Resolution Statistics," Statistic Brain Research Institute, http://www.statisticbrain.com.

*Doing versus being.* We spend our day often rushing from activity to activity or doing various things simultaneously, believing we are multitasking or being effective with our time. We then wonder why we feel we are forgetting things. Perhaps we never gave them our full attention in the first place! Studies in attention show that proper multitasking doesn't exist! Doing various things simultaneously only increases errors and slows down the process. Today and every day, commit to doing one thing at a time. Do it consciously, even enjoy it! What activity did I give my full attention to today? What did I learn by doing it this way?

When we are in the doing mode our concentration is dispersed; we might be thinking of things in the past (most likely, how they should have been) or worrying about how they should or might be in the future. In contrast, in the being mode we are fully present in the moment. When faced with an uncomfortable, unpleasant experience we can be curious and open to it rather than try to avoid it (aversion). Instead of changing things to fit our idea of how they should be, we allow things to be as they are. Accepting with a patient, non-judgmental attitude. This does not mean you should put yourself in painful or dangerous situations, but every now and then go out of your comfort zone and connect with what arises in your bodily sensations, your thoughts (and interpretations), and your emotions.

Example:

1. Doing mode

   Situation: I am made to wait in a queue.

   Sensations: My legs feel tired.

   Thoughts: My boss will be angry if I am late. I am always late. I may lose my job.

   Emotions: Fear.

2. Being mode

   Situation: I am made to wait in a queue.

   Sensations: I have pins and needles in my legs, and my lower back feels hot.

   Thoughts: I cannot help my lateness. I am doing my best.

   Emotions: Acceptance of how things are.

Can you find some examples of your own today:

1. Doing mode

   Situation: _____

   _____

   Sensations: _____

   _____

   Thoughts: _____

   _____

   Emotions: _____

   _____

2. Being mode

   Situation: _____

   _____

   Sensations: _____

   _____

   Thoughts: _____

   _____

   Emotions: _____

   _____

# 4
JANUARY

Instead of dreaming about your next holiday, how about building your own refuge that you can take with you wherever you are! Sounds too good to be true? Read on!

Find a quiet place, switch your phone to do-not-disturb, sit comfortably, and close your eyes. You could set your timer on the phone for 1 minute and add 1 minute more each time you practice.

Congratulations! You've just managed to have a moment of meditation! It's simple but not easy, as our mind is forever working on overdrive. In fact, it's been called the "monkey brain" because it naturally never stays still. That's why we have to train it to be still through meditation. Try to find a convenient time to practice and try incorporating meditation into your day. What was the most difficult thing for me about meditating?

This introductory exercise in mindfulness helps us to do something deliberately, slowly, and with full attention. It can help us to learn to promote mindful eating and a healthier relationship with food. You will need a quiet place and a raisin! First, acquaint yourself with the positions for meditation (p. 405). Then do the Raisin Exercise (p. 407). What did you notice? What do you think the point of this exercise is? How might this exercise help you in other areas of your life?

*Anne noticed, "Since I went into menopause, my hunger seemed to explode. On top of that, when I was stressed, I would lose all notion of being full. The raisin exercise has taught me to really savor my food. I now allow myself a small square of dark chocolate with my coffee as a treat, without making the whole bar disappear!"*

## 6
### JANUARY

The Body-Scan Meditation (p. 411) is usually around 45 minutes, but to get into the habit, you can try a 5-minute body scan first. You will need to find a quiet place to sit or lie down undisturbed. Take a blanket if it is chilly. The Body-Scan Meditation can be quite relaxing, even though that is not its purpose. If you are sleepy, sitting up while keeping your eyes open might help you avoid falling asleep! What are your observations?

Do the Mountain Pose. Become aware of your feet, your balance. If you feel comfortable, close your eyes. Slowly redistribute your weight on one foot, feeling the weight increasing on one foot and lessening on the other. Can you describe your experience?

_____

_____

_____

_____

_____

_____

_____

_____

_____

_____

_____

_____

_____

_____

_____

_____

_____

# 8

*Becoming aware of sensations.* Hot flashes are an unpleasant side effect of menopause caused by falling levels of the female hormone estrogen. Try to tap into hot flashes by making a note of how and when they occur and what your interpretations are.

How does a hot flash feel?

_____

When do they appear?

_____

What was I doing?

_____

What interpretation did I make?

_____

*Doing daily activities with awareness.* Mindfulness has both formal and informal practice. We can perform any mundane activity (brushing our teeth, washing the dishes, etc.) in a mindful manner. Try to be fully mindful in one activity today, becoming aware of all bodily sensations, sounds, smells, tastes, and appearances when performing it. What are my observations? What might be the purpose of bringing awareness to my daily activities?

# 10

During menopause, increased hunger can result in eating more and putting on weight. Try to make clean, healthy food choices—that is, if possible less processed, more organic and free-range food that includes a wide variety of vegetables, lean protein, fiber-rich slow carbohydrates,* small amounts of healthy fats, and calcium-rich foods. When you are eating, try to savor each bite slowly and really tap into the wonderful sight, smell, texture, and color of what you are eating. Being mindful of your hunger and satiety sensations is an important element in keeping an optimal weight. If you wish to lose weight, try to reduce the occasions you allow yourself an extra serving. Keep an eye on the scale and have reasonable-sized jeans to gauge if your weight is fluctuating upward.

*Today and from now on, I make healthy choices. I make mealtimes a peaceful pause in my day to honor the colors, textures, tastes, and smells of my food. I am grateful for these wonderful moments. I listen to my body's messages of hunger and fullness and stop before I am full.*

## THE RAISIN

It looked banal
sitting there in the
pit of my wet palm
like an over-tanned
local on a deserted
beach of sand.

I turned it over,
rolled it around,
squished it with my fingers,
producing a small sound.

I sniffed it very slowly
and held it to the light.
I placed it in between my lips,
keen to take a bite.

I chewed it very softly,
my saliva made it swell.
It reminded me of toffee,
memories began to well.

What was the purpose
of this practice in slow motion,
tapping into thoughts and feelings,
and connecting with emotion.

The problem is we eat too fast,
gobble down our food.
We do not make our pleasure last
and end up in a mood.
This practice doesn't have a goal,
it's just to help us be.
If we do not lose ourselves,
we can live consciously.

*For information on fiber-rich foods, see: www.eatingwell.com/article/289961/top-vegetarian-protein-sources/ and www.uptodate.com/contents/high-fiber-diet-beyond-the-basics#H1.

Next time you feel a hot flash or physical discomfort, try mentally changing the label from "hot flash" to "call for meditation" or even "I'm feeling warm and cosy"! While labels can be useful, and positive, they can also be reductionist and limiting as well as negative. One meditation that can help with perimenopausal and menopausal symptoms is sitting quietly in easy pose, closing the eyes and focusing your gaze (*drishti*) toward the tip of the nose. This is said to balance the pituitary gland, which is like a master gland in the brain. The pituitary gland normally produces follicle-stimulating hormone that prompts ovulation, but it ceases to do so during menopause.

Roll out your yoga mat. Put your pride aside and focus on what you feel. Expand your chest and open your heart. You could try lying on your back with your arms held perpendicular to your torso. Slowly make small, barely perceptible movements to different parts of the body to check for any tension or comfort in different areas. If you are feeling more energetic you could try Cat-Cow Pose, Sphinx Pose, or Warrior II. A restorative pose like Reclining Bound-Angle Pose could be added at the end. What are your observations?

# 12

*Pleasant experience.* Today try to pay attention to any pleasant experience, big or small. Note your different experiences throughout the day on this table.

| WHAT WAS THE EXPERIENCE? | WHAT BODILY SENSATIONS DID YOU FEEL? | EMOTIONS | THOUGHTS |
|---|---|---|---|
| Ex: Had time for a special breakfast today | Relaxed, light body | Happy | It's so good to not feel the stress of rushing to work. |

Try this short experiment. At mealtimes, pause a minute before taking your first bite to take a deep breath, close your eyes, and just tap into your body's sensations. What are your observations?

# 14
JANUARY

*Mind wandering.* You may find during the meditation exercises that your mind is constantly being pulled away from the present moment. Don't beat yourself up, the brain is constantly working, even when we are asleep! Why might the mental time travel of going to the past or present be a problem? Well, when we are elsewhere, we are not in the here and now. We are in the doing mode and not in the being mode that we encountered on January 3 (go back if you need to refresh your memory). Ruminating about the past can lead to depression. Anticipating the future can lead to anxiety. How can we disengage from spontaneous mind travel? Try the following tips:

- Focus on your breathing. Each breath is an opportunity to return to the present moment.
- Use a meditation such as yesterday's 1-minute meditation before meals.
- Do your daily activities giving them your full and undivided attention.

What are your observations?

*Hot flash record.* Hot flashes can come at any moment during the day or night (night sweats). The next time you have one, instead of fighting it, try answering the questions below. Allow the exercise to bring you back to your body.

What is the situation?

_____

What does the heat feel like? Is it constant or fluctuating?

_____

Where do you feel it most?

_____

What emotions accompany it?

_____

Do you have any interpretations, such as "people will think I'm mad"?

_____

# 16
## JANUARY

You may be surprised to see the following exercise as a meditation. But coloring in pictures mindfully can be an informal meditative experience (similar to any in which one is focused and attentive). Have you ever watched a child color? As adults, we tend to deny ourselves enjoyable, meditative experiences like this, thinking that they are a waste of time. But I urge you to try the exercises and express your creativity.

The word "mandala" comes from the Sanskrit word for circle. Mandalas represent unity, wholeness, and infinity, and have been used in spiritual practices in many cultures. The Swiss psychologist Carl Gustav Jung brought them to the West and often used them for self-expression and creativity.

Coloring in mandalas can be a great way to become centered, and it may be self-soothing. It is easier to color in with crayons, but you could also try felt-tip pens, water colors, or ink. Get creative, and while doing so just notice where your mind is from time to time. If your mind wanders, you might be reminded when you make a mistake! Just bring it back gently to the activity, the colors, the sounds, and so on.

Did you know that during menopause teeth and gum health can suffer due to changes in saliva pH and calcium loss? Set an intention to be extra thorough with brushing and flossing your teeth. Brushing teeth can be an excellent time to be mindful of the motion of your wrist, the texture of the toothpaste, its taste, and the sensations in your mouth as you clean every tooth. Three times a day for 3 minutes—you've done 9 minutes of mindfulness practice and your teeth will thank you for it. *Mindfulness is like mental floss!*

# 18

*How to handle mind wandering.* We have already seen that mind wandering is a natural thing for the brain to do, but we can train our attention to be focused on the present moment through formal and informal meditation. During meditation, when you do catch yourself thinking about other things (e.g., your to-do list, a conversation, something you read), let it be an opportunity to come back! Here are the steps:

1. You notice that you have drifted off. Well done! Pat on the back!
2. Name to yourself what you were thinking of—for example, your to-do list, a conversation, facts, a memory—or were you simply drifting into a sequence of random thoughts?
3. Let the thought go.
4. With patience and compassion bring your attention back to your breath.

Each breath is an opportunity to come back to the here and now.

Don't forget, the yoga postures at the back are not sport, even if they have great benefits for your flexibility, posture, and well-being! You can carry on your usual exercise program or take up a sport, but these exercises from the hatha yoga tradition are more a way to explore awareness of your body.

Sun Salutations are a great way to greet the day. If you are new to yoga, try doing one series slowly and deliberately in the morning. Then at night, lying on your back with your legs perpendicular up a wall, sofa, or headboard for a couple of minutes will help relax your body and get it ready for sleep. This posture is known as Half-Inverted Pose, Legs Up a Wall. What are my observations?

# 20
JANUARY

*Thought exercise*: You see a colleague at work and smile at her as you approach. She seems to ignore you and goes into a room. What thoughts go into your mind?

_____

_____

_____

_____

How do these thoughts reflect your usual analysis of a situation?

_____

_____

_____

_____

Would it make any difference if you found out that her boss had just fired her?

_____

_____

_____

_____

*Take-home message*: thoughts are not facts!

*Today and every day, do one thing at a time!* You will not do more by doing various things at the same time. You can outsource or cut corners. Ask for help kindly and clearly.

# 22
## JANUARY

Turn everyday tasks into mindful opportunities. Everyday tasks like doing the dishes or preparing a cup of tea are great examples. Take your time and connect with your body movements, the sounds, and the taste or smell around you. Today, what routine tasks did I turn into mindful opportunities and become more aware of?

What will you nourish your body with today? Buy it, prepare it, and eat it mindfully. Could you give a little silent or spoken word of gratitude to everyone who was involved in helping get the food to your plate? Then try eating in silence, doing nothing else. Chew each mouthful at least ten times and put down your cutlery between mouthfuls. Eat gracefully and delicately even if you are alone! Enjoy the colors, tastes, and textures of healthy meals. Stop before you are full and clear the table mindfully. Once everything is clear, you could offer yourself an herbal tea. It takes about 20 minutes for our digestive system to inform our brain that it is satiated, so often we carry on eating when we should stop.

# 24
JANUARY

*Tibetan proverb: The secret to living well and longer is eat half,*
*walk double, laugh triple, and love without measure.*

Are you noticing the funny events happening in your day? Today, what funny things did I notice?

Check on your New Year's intentions. How are you faring? What got in the way? How could you get back on track?

# 26
JANUARY

How did you react to yesterday's question about your New Year's intentions? What gets in the way? Be patient, be kind with yourself. Each day, each moment, each breath is a chance to start again.

*Whether in a lasting relationship or a new relationship, today I will put aside expectations or goals in my sexual moments with my partner or when I am alone. I will favor sensuality, affection, and tenderness instead.*

Start by getting to know your new body, just like when you were a teenager . . . the beginner's mind can be sexual too! Get to know what gives you pleasure and how to give yourself pleasure. What are your observations?

_____

_____

_____

_____

_____

_____

_____

_____

_____

_____

_____

_____

_____

_____

_____

_____

_____

_____

_____

# 28

Menopause is a time of metamorphosis. Let it be the doorway into your wisdom years. What changes do you notice that suggest you are evolving into a new way of seeing or being?

*Sonja had always been a very attractive lady. She reported in one session how menopause finally allowed her the opportunity to really be taken seriously. She said that for the first time in her life, while still wanting to be attractive, she was happy to be considered as a more matriarchal figure by younger men and with more wisdom to be proud of.*

Break old patterns. Do things differently and see the results. Write down what you can try doing differently today.

1. _____

2. _____

3. _____

4. _____

What did you learn from this exercise?

_____

_____

_____

_____

_____

_____

_____

_____

_____

_____

_____

_____

_____

_____

_____

What are my meditation goals today?

## The Monastery

Time to slow down,
time to forget about time.
Chime, to be here, now.

Learn that it's alright to be slow,
yearn to have nowhere to go.
All those around elsewhere in a rush,
eyes on the phone, in need of a hush.

Stop the noise, the mental chatter,
going through life like a real mad hatter.
It's here, it's now, don't wait,
enjoy the present, it's a blank slate.

Stop heading toward life,
let life come to you.
Sit up in your chair, just enjoy your brew,
put your worries on hold, watch the
    steam,
reach for your senses, life's not a dream.

Deaf ears, try listening!
Honoring when the other is speaking.
Swap seeing for observing,
drop touching, more caressing.

Connect. Now. Here. Look!
Nature is crying to you,
with warm tears of joy and forgiveness,
holding promise of colors and gifts for us.
And anyway . . . what are you really
    running from?
Stop marching to the beat of someone
    else's drum.
You have your own . . . your heart!

Grow you have, now just start!
It's never too late, mark the correct place
    and date,
today, right here, right now,
you're perfect as you are.

Not only is menopause a biologically challenging moment in a woman's life, but other stressors (career moves, having missed the chance to have your own children, nurturing adolescent children, seeing children moving out of the home, caring for aging parents, and so on) add to this. Making mindfulness part of our daily practice through informal and formal meditation can prepare us for life's stressors. In thirteenth-century China the Daoist monk Gao Daokuan (1195–1277) wrote a series of illustrated poems using the metaphor of a wild or untamed horse to represent ordinary consciousness. It was through self-cultivation, especially meditation, that consciousness could be reined in and harnessed.

*In the way a spirited horse must learn to stand on its hooves and move with grace, my breath will reign in my active spirit. With each breath, I come back to the essence of who I am.*

Can you create your own mantra that could guide you through challenging moments? It could be "I am calm, I am patient, I am compassionate" or any short phrase that neutralizes internal negative messages. What is my mantra of the day?

# February

Thoughts like trains,
come and go,
some quietly,
some with clanking carriages,
some avoided and empty,
some heavy with baggage.
Acknowledge them
and let them flow,
they're not all destined for
where you need to go.

It might be fun to climb aboard,
no fixed destination going toward,
with open mind and open heart,
ready for a brand-new start.
But if you do it mindlessly
and find you're not
where you need to be,
it's time to cease this reverie,
and when the right one comes along,
you'll know to you it does belong.
So next time that you're in this station,
just recall your destination,
it might be marked with
"CONCENTRATION"
or be harmless through elimination.
Peace, compassion, unity,
train your thoughts to mastery.

## 1

Chill! Don't sweat menopause. Try taking cooler showers. Get used to the sensation of water a few degrees cooler than you are used to. Smooth on some cream, giving your skin slow, loving, and grateful strokes. What are your thoughts and observations?

*Mood and other influences.* Being mindful is simple but not easy! It needs effort and discipline. Today be aware when you have a difficult conversation or emotions. Be aware if it is other stressors that are influencing your reaction—for example, arguing with someone as you are stuck in a traffic jam and late for an appointment. Don't mix issues or let one source of stress aggravate another situation. What are your remarks?

*Stress and memory.* Under stress, the hormone cortisol is released, which makes it harder for neurons (cells in the brain) to communicate. We find it harder to remember when we are stressed.

 A simple meditation that you can use when overwhelmed by emotion (journal your observations in the space below):

1. Recognize which emotion it is. There are the basic, universal emotions of happiness, sadness, fear, anger, disgust, and surprise, but there are nuances and mixtures of these—for example, sadness and disgust might create remorse.
2. Pause a moment for a deep breath.
3. Observe the quality of the experience, extracting it from the scenario.
4. What are you feeling in your body?
5. Where do you feel it?
6. Let the sensation of the emotion be the object of your meditation.
7. Take a deep breath and slowly exhale.

Meditation does not mean absolute calmness. It allows us a moment to become intimate with our emotions and let them be transformative.

*Emotion and the breath.* Do you know that each emotion has a specific breathing pattern? By becoming conscious of our breathing and breathing calmly, we can affect our emotions, learning, and sleep.

Become aware of your breathing (the speed, length, and intensity of the breath, the posture and muscle tone of your body) and the thoughts and emotions of the moment. How does the breath affect thoughts and feelings, and how do thoughts and feelings affect breath? Note down some observations in the space below from check-ins throughout the day.

## 5

Meditate when you are feeling great . . . and also when you are feeling lousy! 2 minutes . . . 10 minutes . . . 20 minutes, or more. Breathe in, breathe out. Ground your feet and settle against  the back of your chair, or ease your back onto the surface under you (if you are lying down). Breathe in, breathe out. If you are feeling tense, take a deep breath in, tense the muscles, hold the breath, then when you start feeling a need for air, let the breath out with a deep "cannon breath" (with a round mouth making a short burst as you release the air from your mouth). If you are still feeling tense, repeat the process again. As you let your body and mind align and calm, follow your breath.

*Are you mindful or is your mind full?* In this moment, notice where your mind is. Check in again hourly. If your mind is full of distractions, what happens when you bring your attention to that state of distraction?

You might try using certain reminders such as an alarm on your phone or wearing your watch on the opposite wrist to remind yourself to check in with your thoughts periodically. What do you notice? Try to label the kind of thought (criticism, judgment, doing, worry), then blow through your lips as if you are literally blowing the thought away.

# 7

What thoughts are nourishing your mind today? Are they repetitive? Will they become a habit? We are what we train ourselves to focus on and believe in with regular practice. What regular thoughts do you repeat during your day? Catch some of them and write them down.

Be conscious of space today. Driving in traffic, taking public transportation, or being out in nature. Be conscious of your personal space as well as that of other people and objects. When making a movement, be mindful of performing it gently, deliberately, and graciously. When you have time to take a breath consciously, sit down, or do nothing . . . Take a space in your day! How might this change the result of your action?

# 9

"The future tortures us and the past enslaves us.
And there is the reason why the present escapes us."
—GUSTAVE FLAUBERT, *Madame Bovary*

Cherish the positive moments in your day. But let the negative ones teach you something too. What did you learn from today's difficult moments?

_____

_____

_____

_____

_____

_____

_____

_____

_____

_____

_____

_____

_____

_____

_____

_____

_____

_____

_____

_____

# 11

Today, at some point, change your usual pace. If you usually do something fast, try doing it slowly. What do you notice?

Write down five emotions that you felt today. Look up synonyms and antonyms in a dictionary and note some down for each emotion. If you don't know the words, look them up and discover the fine subtlety and nuances of their different meanings. For example:

*anger*     Synonyms:   annoyance, rage, impatience, fury, exasperation

           Antonyms:   enjoyment, cheer, peace, love, ease, kindness


1. _____     Synonyms:   _____

                      Antonyms:   _____


2. _____     Synonyms:   _____

                      Antonyms:   _____


3. _____     Synonyms:   _____

                      Antonyms:   _____


4. _____     Synonyms:   _____

                      Antonyms:   _____


5. _____     Synonyms:   _____

                      Antonyms:   _____

# 13

Over the years, we tend to craft a narrative of who we are, our roles, our experiences, and our family history. What story are you holding on to about yourself? Is this story reductive? What could be another facet to this story?

"Wherever you are, be there totally."
—ECKHART TOLLE, *The Power of Now*

What could this quotation mean for you today? When is it difficult for you to "be there" totally?

_____

_____

_____

_____

_____

_____

_____

_____

_____

_____

_____

_____

_____

_____

_____

_____

_____

_____

# 15

During menopause, women with a history of depression and anxiety may experience an increase in negative mental states. Rumination (thinking the same negative thoughts over and over) may increase, especially if sleep is disrupted and bodily sensations change for the worse. It is important to remember that thoughts may seem real, but they are not tangible. They are interpretations born of our conditioning. You are not your thoughts. In fact, a *lojong* (mind training) slogan says, "Consider your thoughts as if they were dreams." Catch your thoughts today and become aware of how often you take your thoughts for reality.

Connect with the sensations of a part of your body. Note what you feel: temperature, pressure, tingling, and so on.

# 17

*Ignite your agni!* One way to activate our agni prana (compare this to an inner furnace in our belly) is the "breath of fire" exercise. It might seem paradoxical that just when you wish to turn the heat down rather than up, this exercise is suggested! However, "breath of fire" done a few minutes every day allows you to flush your skin with oxygen (giving you the best glow possible), strengthen your nerves, expand your lungs, and purify your blood. To do this, sit in easy pose; close your eyes; and maintain an equal, strong inbreath and outbreath that emanates from a pumping navel.

PC . . . politically correct? No, pelvic conditioning! OK, sisters. There's something that has to be braced, and today is as good a day as any. We're talking about the pelvic floor: the deep, muscular tissues and ligaments that support our reproductive organs, the rectum, and the bladder.

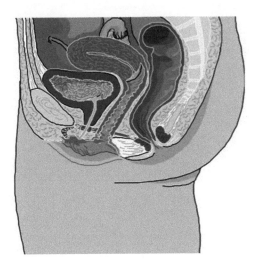

These muscles weaken over the years with childbirth, age, and gravity. I am going to propose to you a series of exercises that you should ideally do 2–3 times per week, and much more if possible! What might this have to do with mindfulness, you may ask? Well, the exercises have to be done with the breath. The idea is to take a long, deep abdominal breath in. Hold it a few seconds, then slowly exhale while pulling up the pelvic floor muscles as if you are stopping your flow of urine, holding a few seconds, and releasing as you breathe in. With time you can squeeze more and more and visualize the different parts of your organs as you perform the exercises. You can do this anywhere (sitting, standing in a queue) and anytime, while being conscious of the sensations. Let it be your mindfulness Kegel exercises. At home you can do them in bed before drifting off to a quiet slumber. This exercise will improve continence and sexuality, and it will help you gain awareness of this important area of your body.

# 19

*Menopause, memory, and mindfulness.* Brain fog (loss of memory and concentration) is a common symptom of menopause. Many women worry whether it is a sign of mild cognitive impairment. Although this brain fog is temporary, one way to combat it is to learn something new every day. What did you learn today, however big or small?

*Menopause, stress, and speed.* Menopause is a time of accelerated aging due to slower regeneration. For this reason, overcommitment, speed, and business just tax the body further through stress. Today's practice is to observe how speed affects your daily life and your practice. How does being faster or slower and first or last make you feel? Try changing the speed at which you usually might do things (including driving too fast) and see how your perspective, emotions, and level of enjoyment changes.

# 21

Later on in the week you will need body oil, so please put that on your shopping list. I recommend clary sage essential oil and fractionated coconut oil.

*Choose a yoga sequence and do it mindfully. You might try some lower backbend poses such as Cobra, Bow, or Bridge. These help keep the spine flexible, tone the kidneys, and relieve tension and tiredness.*

*Healthy social networks and a healthy brain.* Staying socially active is important for cognitive health. Very often, we can be self-critical and critical of others. This makes social interaction difficult. Mindfulness teaches us to be compassionate with ourselves and others. Today, be conscious of these criticisms and judgments in your head.

## 23
### FEBRUARY

When we first learn a skill, we give it our undivided attention. Where does your mind go when you are doing something automatic, as when reading, drawing, or driving?

Color in the mandala below. Be conscious of your posture, breathing, and thoughts, and of the textures of the crayons and even the sounds they make while you are coloring. Where does your mind go, and what judgments go through your mind?

*How is your love life?* Do you know that keeping your sexuality alive is important for your well-being and for your intimate relationship? Focusing on negative thoughts during sex is a big passion killer. Just like during meditation when your mind wanders, try to return to the breath. Feel each muscle individually with each breath. If you find a part of your body is tense, breathe and loosen it. Let sex be a path to knowledge about yourself and your partner. Allow sex to be a time to focus on your mind, body, and spiritual connection.

# 25
## FEBRUARY

*Menopause, tolerance, and comfort!* Mindfulness invites us to be tolerant and accept being out of our comfort zone when it cannot be avoided. However, menopause is a life stage that allows us to really dig deep and make choices that provide us with the physical comfort we need more than ever before. For example, I have found the pleasure of wearing natural fabrics against my skin and have become far less tolerant of compromising my comfort for fashion! What choices have you made today to provide yourself with comfort? Are these healthy for you in the long run?

Draw yourself a warm bath. You could add some Epsom salts (great for soothing tired muscles), a teaspoon of honey (a natural skin humectant and a carrier), and a few drops of your favorite essential oil (lavender, for example, is very relaxing) to the honey and salt. Mix them together well and mix into the bathwater until dissolved. Light some candles and turn off the lights. Allow yourself at least 20 minutes to just enjoy the temperature, the perfume, the sounds, and everything else that your senses can tap into. How was the experience?

# 27

Do a yoga sequence—for example, some Sun Salutations. Be aware of what thoughts go through your mind as you adopt the postures. Do you tend to respect your body, stopping when there is pain? Do you allow yourself a pause if you are very tired? Do you carry on or stop too quickly the moment it gets challenging? What did you notice?

Declining estrogen levels during menopause can cause havoc with emotions, ranging from mild mood swings to severe depression. Fear and worry might also get worse. Unfortunately, these emotional changes are a normal part of menopause. Look at the wheel of emotions in the image below.* Make a mental note of the range of emotions you have experienced today.

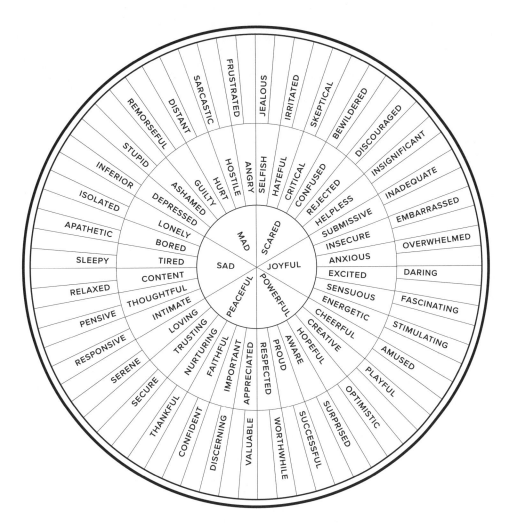

*Janet sometimes feels that she has constant PMT. Looking at the wheel of emotions and noting what had triggered certain emotions and where they were coming from in her body helped her to see patterns. Learning to take the time and distance needed to digest them and to take care of herself (even with a few gentle breaths) made the roller coaster feeling more bearable for her.*

What emotions are you experiencing right now? Try this throughout the day and see how these emotions change. What drives these emotions?

*"The Feelings Wheel," developed by Dr. Gloria Willcox.

# March

She no longer needs
to let her blood drain
every month like
hunted wild game.
Reminded of lost opportunities,
her soul has won a new immunity
to soar to new heights,
light as a kite,
a passage of right.

Do the Mountain Pose. Then do the Palm Tree Pose. See how long and how steady you can be. If the poses are challenging, you can use a wall or the back of a chair to help you maintain balance. What are your observations?

_____

_____

_____

_____

_____

_____

_____

_____

_____

_____

_____

_____

_____

_____

_____

_____

_____

_____

_____

_____

*Breast friends.* Breasts! Yes, we women have a bittersweet relationship with ours. What greater reminder can nature give us of the impermanence of life than our own breasts, which we experience as ever changing—at puberty, at different times of the menstrual cycle, during pregnancy and while breastfeeding, when we lose and put on weight! Very few women are happy with the size and shape of their breasts, not to mention their nipples!

But I think we should embrace our breasts however they are. Tonight, after your shower or bath, take an extra minute to massage them with scented oil (1/4 cup of fractionated coconut oil, 2 drops of clary sage essential oil, and 2 drops of peppermint essential oil is a great combo and delightfully refreshing), and take time to honor them. This should be part of your routine or a ritual in which you give thanks to your uniqueness, and that includes your "boobs and bumps"!

This kind self-care allows you to check your breasts and be in tune with your sensuality: Start at the armpit, go down the side of the body and then massage toward the nipple. Radiate your fingers from each nipple as if drawing lines outward, or going around a clock twice with your oiled fingers, each time toward the armpit. This helps lymphatic drainage and increases fresh blood supply to the area. While doing this, visualize it as a caring, cleansing, and healing gesture. Tap into the sensations of different parts of your breasts.

# 3

How did you handle stressful moments today? What would you like to improve?

_____

_____

_____

_____

_____

_____

_____

_____

_____

_____

_____

_____

_____

_____

_____

_____

_____

_____

_____

_____

_____

_____

We tend to think that our take on our environment and situation is a true rendition of reality, but did you know that most of our perception of reality is predicted, constructed, filtered, filled in, neglected, and often distorted? It is just the way the human brain manages the constant and enormous inflow of information. Knowing that we are all prone to cognitive biases and mental shortcuts can help us remain humble in our certitude of being "right." Let every situation be what it is, instead of what you think it is.

**MARCH**

Check your use of the phone while talking to someone else. You cannot be there and be on your phone! You cannot blame your menopausal memory if you never gave the moment your full attention in the first place! Have certain times of the day to check emails and mobile phones so that they don't become a constant interruption. If in doubt about the frequency of your use, download a free app and monitor how often and how much time you spend on your phone. You may be surprised!

*Sleep and Menopause.* How are you sleeping? Did you know that getting sufficient sleep is important for weight management, cardiovascular health, cognitive function, sexual function, mood, and a host of other health-related functions? Become conscious of your wind-down routine, stopping the use of screen technology around 9 pm and giving yourself time to tap into the feelings of your need for rest.

When you are ready for sleep, lying down on your left side is said to promote left-nostril breathing, which relaxes the body. Close your eyes and concentrate on your inbreath and outbreath in the left nostril. Try to guide your outbreath to be just a little longer than the inbreath.

# 7

Today is International Women's Day! The official logo of the day is the symbol of Venus, and the color is purple. Pick out something purple to wear today. Each time you look at it, pause and give thanks to the women in your life who have forged who you are today.

Do the Body-Scan Meditation (p. 411).

What sensations did you feel in your body?

# 9

What thoughts are you nourishing in this moment? Is this a familiar pattern? Is this pattern helping you to be serene?

Remember your New Year's intention? How are you getting on with it? Might you need to revise your intentions and remind yourself what small changes could help you build new good habits? For example, if losing some excess weight was one of them, you could make one small change to get nearer to your goal, such as adding a portion of fresh vegetables to your meal or cutting down on processed food.

# 11

"The real meditation is how you live your life."
—Jon Kabat-Zinn, *Wherever You Go, There You Are*

In other words, use mindfulness to fully experience your life. What could you plan to do mindfully today? This evening, or tomorrow, come back and note how bringing mindful awareness to the situation altered the experience for you.

_____

_____

_____

_____

_____

_____

_____

_____

_____

_____

_____

_____

_____

_____

_____

_____

_____

Did you know that owning a cat or dog helps relieve stress, improve mood, and increase our opportunities for exercise?* If you don't own a dog, why not help a neighbor by taking their dog for a walk when you are free? In my opinion, walking a dog and being at one with its curiosity, joy, and enthusiasm is one of the best meditations out there!

Bailey is the most mindful dog—he lives in the present and never worries about the past or the future!

Practice the Downward-Facing Dog Pose today. Like a loyal dog returning to your practice day after day, bring these qualities of loyalty, presence, love, and determination to your practice. What are your thoughts when doing this exercise?

_____

_____

_____

_____

_____

_____

_____

_____

_____

_____

_____

_____

_____

*Evanson and Simon, "Clarifying the Relationship between Parenthood and Depression," 341–58; Siegel et al., "AIDS Diagnosis and Depression in the Multicenter AIDS Cohort Study," 157–70.

Look out for what you might be resisting today.

When you get into bed, take five deep breaths in through the nose and out of the mouth. Feel the contact of your body with the mattress and the contact of your skin with the sheets. Can you whisper to yourself three words of gratitude at being who you are, where you are at this moment in life?

Set an intention to meditate a little every day—a minute a few times a day is great, as is a longer period if you can. Close your eyes, connect with your breath and bodily sensations. Notice any emotions. Even though we might find it easier and think it is a "better meditation" when we are calm and have plenty of time, in fact committing to a regular practice in tough times is great training. It's like becoming a skilled and confident sailor by venturing out on increasingly rougher waters.

Because sweating might increase during menopause, be mindful to drink enough water every day to avoid dehydration, which might cause the similar symptoms that you are trying to avoid—brain fog, palpitations, hunger and dizziness, and dry, itchy skin, to name a few. A water filter makes the practice pure and ecological. Aim for about 1.5 to 2 liters. If you are not used to drinking enough water, start slowly, perhaps adding an extra glass a day. Invest in a nice, leakproof bottle that you can carry around with you. You can add fresh herbs, cut fruit, or herbal tea bags to the water in a flask or bottle and drink it throughout the day.

Allow this moment to be a time for you to take stock of any build-up of tension in your body. Breathe deeply through the nose. Drink mindfully, observing the taste, the temperature, and the sensation of the water on your tongue and throat as you swallow it. Give thanks to having access to clean, fresh water and think of it hydrating your cells.

*Mindful walking.* Put on comfy shoes and clothes. Leave your phone behind! Go for a walk, taking it at a slower pace than usual. Drink in the sights, sounds, and sensations of your surroundings. You can even try your hand at poetry, as I did below while on a mindfulness retreat. I had never written poetry before, but being silent and having time for quiet contemplation enabled me to tap into my creativity. You might want to take a pen and pad with you to note down sounds as they come!

## SPRING

A competition—
as birds premiere
their renditions of "Spring."

A bee, a miniature
overloaded military aircraft,
its trajectory internally photographed.

A lizard jolting for refuge
at the sound of a
step that's huge.

Footsteps crunching on cool gravel,
toasting in the sun,
walking on a bed of cornflakes—
time travel, there is none.

Bells of distant cows
sound as heavy as their udders.
The tractor through the ground it
    ploughs,
breaking through the mud.
A door bangs,
another episode begun.

A toy car
wending its way down
the mountain road,
far from where you are.

A small plane crossing the path,
its shadow an acrobat,
of the silent one above,
insignificant as a gnat.

A kicked stone flies forward,
a meteorite to the ant,
who takes the brunt—
a small life altered.

A distant bark,
like an exclamation mark,
foiling another raid
that the postman might have made.

A cockerel going off—
the time is unusual,
he may be delusional,
but still it is quite beautiful.

A crow communicating in the
    vernacular,
ebony spectacular.
A man interrupting nature
on his phone, head bent down,
a worried portraiture.

A buzz of electricity . . .
a noisy necessity.

Pressurized water
spewing its contents onto the floor,
like angry gore.

Another propeller plane,
into the unknown it sails.

A bird sounding its maracas,
adding to the fracas—
a burst into symphony,
a crescendo to nature
and manifestation of harmony.

Put your legs up! This Half-Inverted Pose, Legs Up a Wall (p. 446) allows your heartbeat to slow down and aids restoration. Lie near a wall, your buttocks as near as possible to the edge. Put your feet up the wall, legs straight. Spend 5 minutes with your eyes closed. Watch the natural rhythm of your breath. Enjoy.

What did you discover from this position? Where there any difficulties? What delights did you find in the posture?

# 18

Thoughts are not facts! Don't fight them, get lost in them, or get rid of them. Just watch them like clouds drifting across the sky! Try to do it a few times today.

Would the mountain be so magnificent
if it had not withstood
the titanic pressures
forcing it to move?
Would it hold its head so proudly
were it not for staying put
when hit by wind and ice and rain,
taking each day as a blessing?

Today is the first day of spring. Take a walk and really notice the trees, grass, and flowers as if you were a detective.

_____

_____

_____

_____

_____

_____

_____

_____

_____

_____

_____

_____

_____

_____

_____

## 20
### MARCH

Hormones such as ghrelin, leptin, adiponectin, and insulin affect appetite. Levels of ghrelin and adinopectin increase during menopause. Before you rush to quell sensations of hunger, tap into these sensations. Wait patiently until mealtimes. If you are hungry before mealtime, try drinking more water, herbal tea, or infused water, as quite often your body mistakes dehydration signals for hunger.

Do the Body-Scan Meditation (p. 411).

What are your observations?

# 22
MARCH

In mindfulness, the impermanence of life events is recognized. If we stay calm and mindful when facing pain or discomfort, we will see that on most occasions, it passes.

This can be useful when we are experiencing a hot flash.

*Emily experiences a hot flash at work when talking with her boss. She feels distressed, fearful that he will see her sweating, and thinks, "this hot flash is lasting forever . . . he will think I am really stressed." She retreats to her office and feels very angry.*

*Julie feels a hot flash coming and focuses on taking slow, deep breaths. She knows it won't last long before it's over. She takes five deep, slow breaths in and out, telling herself that she is "coming home" within her inner retreat with each breath. At the end of her breathing, she feels the hot flash is passing.*

In mindfulness practice people and nature are seen as interrelated and interconnected. The notion of a separate, independent entity is considered an illusion. For this reason, over-attachment, whether to situations, thoughts, habits, objects, beliefs, or others, is considered a root of unhappiness. To whom or what are you clinging or holding on? What would it mean to let go of the result and enjoy the process? How might this be relevant to you at this precious junction of your life?

# 24

*Love.* How can you show altruistic love today to the people in your life and those who cross your path with your attitude, presence, and awareness? How can your partner show you their love? How can you show yourself love today?

## AMOUR

You have shown me,
allowed me to know
what romantic love can really be,
not a show.
I am so grateful for that, you see—
to realize I can rely on you,
when life I have to just plod through.

Love's not about how long it lasts,
our color, language, wealth, or class,
nor even at which age we meet,
love at first sight or that starts discrete.

To think of you throughout my day,
when in dismay we run the rat race.
One day, life will tear us from each
     other's embrace
like a hardened hunter plucking an
     animal prematurely from its mother.
Our choked cries too will go unheard.

But today, I carry you in my heart like
     a delicate lotus,
a work of art that can so easily be
     destroyed
instead of honored and enjoyed.
Knowing that words nourished on
     anger and hate
can shear bones and harm and love
     frustrate,
leaving a scar that may forever be ajar.

Today, right here, right now,
to you the best of me I vow.
Consider you with thoughts and
     actions delicately,
kind intentions and trusting sensuality.

Fit some yoga into your day. If you can do 5 minutes, well done. If you finish the whole sequence, congratulations! What are your observations?

# 26
MARCH

Negative thoughts: each time you have a negative thought, observe it, name it, and let it go.

_____

_____

_____

_____

_____

_____

_____

_____

_____

_____

_____

_____

_____

_____

_____

_____

_____

_____

_____

_____

_____

Life is about learning and growing from our experiences. We have so many opportunities to make a fresh start . . . each day is a new beginning. What three lessons did today bring you?

# 28

MARCH

Surrender to what is. Let go of what was. Have faith in what will be.

Constipation can increase during menopause as intestinal motility decreases. In addition, stress alters the way we breathe, making it shallow and fast, instead of slow, deep, and from the belly, which helps massage the intestines. Another problem is that women are often shy to go to the toilet in public places or choose to ignore the whispers from their body that it is time to answer nature's call if the time is not convenient. So today commit extra attention to digestion. This starts with proper breathing, listening to our bodily urges, and if possible trying some of the poses in the yoga section that aid digestion, such as Cow-Face Pose on page 430, or Wind-Relief/Knee-to-Chest Pose and Reclined Spinal Twist on page 442.

These yoga postures are also a beneficial remedy for constipation. Listen to your body and don't force yourself into a posture if it is painful. Take the postures slowly. Hold each one and breathe slowly and deeply, giving your digestive organs an inner massage. Which yoga poses were you able to try? What are your observations?

## 30
MARCH

*Give me attitude!* Right attitude is one of the keys to mindfulness. How can we be curious, open-minded, kind, and compassionate? When is it easiest to have the right attitude? With which people is it easy to have the right attitude, and when is it hardest? When it is hard to have the right attitude, what might be behind it? Fear, pride, disappointment, or something else?

When is it difficult to be mindful? Check which of these mindful qualities are particularly challenging in difficult times:

- ☐ Patience
- ☐ Compassion
- ☐ Non-judgment
- ☐ Equanimity
- ☐ Calm
- ☐ Beginner's mind

# April

### THE SYCAMORE TREE

The sycamore tree knew it all,
it had seen kings and countries rise
    and fall.
It stood there majestic, strong, and tall,
knowing that life's not always a ball.

It gave of itself with a generous tone,
parachuting its seeds safely to the
    ground
on the lawn waiting patiently could they
    be found
and asking for nothing in return
but some rays of the sun.
A sprinkle of rain, and so it had begun,
its journey through time,
respecting the seasonal rhyme,
in Summer bestowing its shade,
one branch strong for a swing it made.

It looked down to the valley,
watching the town, its pace like a rally.
bowing to the winds with dignity,
surrendering with compassion
during a dry spring.

Silence had taught it to adapt,
when carved by lovers,
crying tears of joy
with its sap.

Oh people, I wish you would know
that I am waiting come sun or snow—
come lie under me,
for you will see,
I have enough arms
to make all of you calm.

My fingers are delicate, heal your
    frenzy with my balm—
come be with me,
feel my energy,
under the green
that I have to give,
just be still
and really start to live.

When we are in the being mode we are aware of what we are doing. We are less in the doing mode, the mind wanders less—in other words, we are less on automatic pilot. It is easier to slip into depression and anxiety when we are on automatic pilot. Be aware today when you are in the being or doing (automatic pilot) mode.

Today, when was I in the being mode? When was I on autopilot? How do I feel when in the autopilot doing mode? What differences do I feel when in the being mode?

*June arrived at work. She had a hard time remembering what route she had taken. She worried that her memory was not what it used to be. She had taken a few calls and sipped her coffee at the same time, while wondering when she would go to the supermarket and what she would cook tonight.*

*Daniela made a conscious effort to be present as she drove to work. She gave herself extra time to enjoy the drive. She felt the temperature of the cool steering wheel in her hands and paid extra attention to the rising sun, which looked particularly spectacular as the lake was smooth that morning. At the traffic light, she took a deep, conscious breath in and out.*

Do a 3-minute meditation at some point today. If you can, repeat the exercise a few times throughout the day. What are your observations?

Let's think about company today. Who would like your company today? What do they value in your company? Whose company would you value today? Could you express that to them, and what it is about them that you appreciate? Are you generous with your company? Do you enjoy your own company?

Today I would like you to pay attention to reactivity (which can get worse when our hormones are unstable, we are sleep-deprived, and hot and bothered!). How do you react when something annoys or disappoints you? Frustrations are a normal part of life, but how we react to them is our choice. Very often we forget or ignore the fact that people, like us, have their own problems and frustrations, and sometimes more than we do.

Do a 3-minute meditation at some point today on recognizing anger and irritation. How does it manifest in your body, and what thoughts accompany the feelings? You may put your hands onto your sternum, one over the other, while you close your eyes and meditate. Focus on compassion and invite it into your meditation. Can you think of someone who is calm, wise, and compassionate? How can you respond rather than react?

**5**

APRIL

*Mindful walking.* Do the mindful walking meditation (p. 410). What might walking in this way teach you?

110

Spend some time thinking about who you would like to be (not someone famous, but your best and realistic version), and maybe ask someone close to you how they would describe you. What is holding you back from being who you would like to be? What can you let go of in order to be that person?

# 7

Plan a practice of your choice for today. What are your observations?

_____

_____

_____

_____

_____

_____

_____

_____

_____

_____

_____

_____

_____

_____

_____

_____

_____

_____

_____

_____

_____

_____

Did you do your intended practice yesterday? If not, why was it difficult to accomplish it? What might be done to reduce these kinds of difficulties? Might you try it today without the obstacle?

# 9
## APRIL

"For we women are not only the deities of the household fire
but the flame of the soul itself."

—Rabindranath Tagore, *The Home and the World*

Kinda, a forty-nine-year-old woman said in therapy that as time went by she had regrets. They stemmed from her realization that in order to not bother her partner, she had never asked or expected him to celebrate special occasions (such as the day they met). In fact, her birthday had never been celebrated when she was growing up. However, she longed to have her partner celebrate these dates. We spoke about how she might better recognize her needs and desires, about her right to evolve new desires and needs over time, and about how she could communicate them to her partner, who might in fact be delighted to make her happy.

Are you in tune with your needs, desires, and dreams? Do you welcome them into your life, or do you judge them, dismiss them, shut them down, or bypass them? What would you write in the space below to complete these: I would love my partner to . . . I need to feel . . . My needs are . . .

Go on a "wonder walk" and open your eyes to all the miracles you encounter. How can you observe the world today with loving eyes, listen with loving ears, see the beauty in every situation? Make a note of what you observed.

# 11

*Handy mindfulness.* After menopause, falling estrogen levels can lead to pigmented skin, swelling joints and ligaments, and stiffness that can cause hand pain. Nails can become brittle too. Today become aware of your hands, how they feel the textures and temperatures of things you hold; the strength of your hands, but also how delicate they are. Can you give them a little extra loving attention, such as a gentle scrub with some basic kitchen ingredients (coconut oil, brown sugar, sea salt, and oats)? After rinsing them and patting them dry, slather on hand cream and give yourself a gentle hand massage. Don't forget to protect your hands from harmful sun rays with an SPF cream when you are outdoors. Let this become a moment to practice self-care and connecting to such an important part of your body.

*June lost the use of her right hand after a motorcycle accident. She said she had taken her hands for granted all her life. For a moment stop to imagine how challenging life would be without your hands and how much they do for you.*

Plan an outing and really be in the moment. It could be a trip to a botanical garden, a museum, a concert, any religious building, or an animal shelter. Go there with an open mind and heart. What are your observations? You may draw or doodle your emotions, thoughts, or feelings too. Be aware of any self-judgments when doing this exercise.

Mindfulness is not about having no thoughts. Mindfulness is about having them, recognizing them, not getting wrapped up in them, and being serene in the process.

Hormonal fluctuations may worsen headaches during perimenopause, although women who suffered from premenstrual headaches may find they decrease after menopause. Tension can definitely make headaches worse. Could you try observing where your thoughts are a few times a day, taking a slow, deep inbreath and outbreath and doing a few slow head rolls—as if you are drawing a circle on the ceiling with your head?

Think about three things today concerning your age that you are grateful for, journaling your thoughts in the space below.

# 15

Sometimes we must let go of past objects, stages, and situations in order to make room for the new. This week pack a bag of things that you no longer need, that do not fit you, or that you don't feel good wearing. Give them to charity, sell them, or throw them away if they are unusable. What feelings are stirred in you by this action?

_____

_____

_____

_____

_____

_____

_____

_____

_____

_____

_____

_____

_____

_____

_____

_____

_____

_____

_____

_____

_____

What are you experiencing right now, here where you are?

# 17

Invite a friend to go on a 5-minute silent mindfulness meditation walk with you. Become aware of your movements, surroundings, emotions, and thoughts. Afterward, discuss what you experienced, allowing each other 5 minutes to express your experience while the other listens carefully in silence.

Feeling "catty"? Irritability tends to be a common symptom of menopause. What activities or practices help you feel peaceful? One yoga pose that can be beneficial is the Lion Pose. Look up the instructions (p. 433) and have fun doing this pose at some point today. What did you notice?

# 19
APRIL

Close your eyes and give gratitude for five things in your week, journaling your thoughts in the space below.

Yesterday, you were asked to do a gratitude exercise. Did you know that feeling gratitude reduces your heart rate and arousal levels and activates the brain's "mu opioid" networks, which mediate positive reinforcement? Mu receptors are like minute locks on our neurons (brain cells) that receive keys (compounds) that decrease pain.

# 21
## APRIL

*Take a hike!* Are you aware of "nature therapy"? Being in nature has a wonderful effect on our physical, emotional, spiritual, and mental health. Set the intention to go offline—no phone, no planning. Now find a lush, green place. If possible, a place that has a particularly uplifting effect on you. Bring your attention to the present moment. Check in on your breathing, your bodily sensations, and your experience of the environment. Let the sounds, sights, smells, and sensations come to your eyes, ears, nose, skin, muscles, and so on. When your mind wanders, gently bring it back to your breath or one of your senses.

Reconnect with the environment. If possible, repeat this experience during different seasons. It is a fantastic way to reconnect with the cycles of life, death, and rebirth. Become aware of the paradox of change and consistency.

As we get older, the thought of our death or the death of older family members may become more real. Become conscious today of the impermanence of life. How might this influence your behavior with close family members, friends, and colleagues?

Be conscious of your breath when you are stressed. The breath is the best way to regulate emotions!

Incorporate some yoga poses into your routine. One way to regulate our stress levels with our breathing is by trying to reduce the number of inhales and exhales a minute. Ideally, try six or eight breaths a minute. Breathe very slowly through the nose and try to fill the lungs. Then pause a second or two and, with the lips pursed, let the air come out slowly, as if you were blowing through a straw or even whistling, until you run out of exhalation. When your lungs are empty, pause a second or two and start again. What are your observations?

Take it easy. Very often we rush to catch the next train or break speed limits when in fact there is no urgency! If there is, poor time management might be the cause. Give yourself time to get to your appointments in a calm manner and enjoy the journey there. If you are not able to do that, why might you feel a need to rush? How are things different when done in a rush or when done slowly and purposefully? If you simply tend to take on too much, how might you cut down?

# 25
APRIL

What are your fears about menopause? What physical sensations accompany these fears?

Sleep can become more fragmented and lighter during menopause. If you wake up in the night, what goes through your mind? Next time, try focusing on slowly and rhythmically tensing and relaxing different parts of your body. Then reconnect to the rhythmic, natural quality of the breath. Allow sleeplessness to offer you the perfect moment for a meditation.

# 27
APRIL

Your attitude during yoga poses are a reflection of your attitude generally. When you get into a posture, check your expectations, recriminations, anger, or how soon you give up. Yoga is as much about mental flexibility as physical flexibility!

"We never know the worth of water until the well is dry."

—Thomas Fuller (source unknown)

Mindfulness activities done today:

☐ Meditation

☐ Yoga

☐ Informal practice

# 29
APRIL

What is going well today? This is important for me because . . . What was challenging today?

When people annoy you, recognize that:

- ✦ the world is an imperfect place
- ✦ people are imperfect
- ✦ you are imperfect

Embrace these thoughts with all the kindness and compassion you can muster.

# May

I walk this path
like the women before me,
hovering between youth
and old age.
They came from the water,
ancestral cradle,
beckoning each daughter.
Rhythmic call,
an invitation
to meditation
finer than any tingsha bell.

# 1

As often as you can and when practical, stop what you are doing, close your eyes, and just be.

_____

_____

_____

_____

_____

_____

_____

_____

_____

_____

_____

_____

_____

_____

_____

_____

_____

_____

_____

_____

_____

Try to make a point of spending a few minutes every day surrounded by trees, plants, and flowers. Being surrounded by nature makes me . . .

_____

_____

_____

_____

_____

_____

_____

_____

_____

_____

_____

_____

_____

_____

_____

_____

_____

_____

_____

## 3
**MAY**

What helped me to be mindful today?

Commit to taking the stairs when you can. Be mindful of your bodily sensations, movements, and thoughts as you do this exercise.

# 5
MAY

Find a small space in your home where you can dedicate some time to meditating without being interrupted, even a small area under a staircase. It can have a low table, a few ornaments, some interesting stones or pebbles, a plant, some cushions, and a candle. Now that you have dedicated the physical space, make a habit of coming here once a day to sit down and check in with yourself. A sand-timer might help you stick to a timed session.

Next time you are feeling emotionally reactive, remember the acronym STOP:*

1. **S**top.
2. **T**ake a couple of breaths. This will calm the sympathetic nervous system.
3. **O**bserve in a compassionate manner your thoughts, emotions, and bodily sensations. Don't try to change them or justify them. Just welcome what arises with a gentle curiosity. Don't fall for your internal dialogue that may convince you how right you are in reacting. Don't react.
4. **P**erspective is essential. In being with what is, without reactivity, you create the space to see the situation clearly and let your natural intelligence step in. Within this space, creative and compassionate solutions can emerge for all those involved.

*Stahl and Goldstein, *A Mindfulness-Based Stress Reduction Workbook*.

# 7
## MAY

Hone in on five wonderful views when you are outside today. What do you see?

1. _____

2. _____

3. _____

4. _____

5. _____

What thoughts and feelings did these views evoke?

_____

_____

_____

_____

_____

_____

_____

_____

_____

_____

_____

_____

_____

_____

_____

_____

As we get older we learn to juggle many balls. I have noticed that one way to avoid stress and to enjoy the moment is by being early! However, at the beginning, especially when you have gotten used to being very efficient and overscheduling, those empty periods in which you are waiting may sometimes feel like a waste of time. Next time you have something to do, check your time management. If you are late, what are the real reasons? Were you trying to squeeze in a few extra chores or activities? Could they not have waited? Could you not have delegated?

As women, our work will NEVER be all done. As we get older, the weight of responsibility for our younger and older family members can burden us even more, so accept that you will do what you can but not everything on your to-do-list will get done. Enjoy being early and sometimes just having the opportunity to wait (breathe, drink water, admire your surroundings, people watch, and so on).

*As I wait for my boat to cross Lake Leman to go to work, it gives me an opportunity to admire the serenity of the landscape and the mirrorlike stillness of the water.*

How does waiting make me feel?

_____

_____

_____

_____

_____

_____

_____

_____

_____

_____

_____

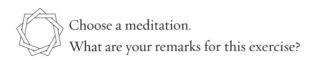

Choose a meditation.

What are your remarks for this exercise?

### RENAISSANCE

A new breath,
a new beginning,
ever evolving
in form and being,
connected, not separate,
interconnected, interbeing.

Not today,
who I was yesterday,
labels fall,
name changes,
I am more than
a woman,
a mother,
a colleague,
a student,
a neighbor,
a daughter,

a sister,
a mistress,
a temptress . . .

A new me,
an opportunity.
Elements ejected,
elements injected.
New atoms in every cell,
belonging here,
belonging there,
everywhere,
and nowhere,
the cosmos
inside of me.
A wise, mature woman,
I am free to be me.

Do a meditation practice of your choice. Try to be aware of cravings, daydreaming, or fantasizing that may come as intrusive thoughts. These distract us from being present to the situation. Just note when they arise and be aware of what you might be trying to avoid. What are your observations?

*This was Patricia's observation as she meditated today: "While doing my meditation practice today, I realized I kept thinking about food. I was hungry and impatient to get my practice out of the way. Then I felt guilty about not being a good meditator. I realized this was an opportunity to bring myself back to the present and be less judgmental, and that my food cravings pass."*

# 11
MAY

How is it right now? Right here. Stop to ask yourself this question several times a day, honing in on your thoughts, bodily sensations, emotions. Don't enter into the eye of the storm of your attention, but observe. So if you realize that you are sad, notice the sadness without getting caught up in the reasons, your justification, and so on. If you feel sad, instead of saying, "I am sad," reframe it as "There is some sadness."

As you wake up today, take a few minutes to connect to the sensations of your skin against the sheets. Take a deep breath in and slowly let it out. Set an intention for the day. It could be caring for your body, being at peace with this phase of your life, or showing kindness to those you interact with. You might write your intention down on small post-it notes and put the notes in visible places. At the end of the day, check in and see how much you managed to stick to your intention. What was difficult about it? Plan repeating the exercise with the same, an updated, or a new intention for tomorrow. We construct our lives out of small daily choices.

# 13

Change perspective—in your thoughts, reactions, habits, and routes. Just do it! Note the differences. What did you learn?

_____

_____

_____

_____

_____

_____

_____

_____

_____

_____

_____

_____

_____

_____

_____

_____

_____

_____

_____

_____

_____

Set your telephone to make a small noise every hour—let's say between the moment you wake up until you go to sleep (except when you are in meetings or need to be offline). When it rings, notice if you are on autopilot (the mode in which you are doing something you are used to and are accomplished at, while daydreaming of something else) or if you are truly aware and giving your full attention without letting your mind wander elsewhere. What are the qualia of each of these moments?

# 15

Do you know that dancing is a great way to keep mentally and physically fit in a fun, sociable way? Are there any types of dancing that you have always dreamed of learning? Could you invite your partner, friend, or family member to try a new dance class or just go alone and dance with other singles? What thoughts accompany this suggestion?

My women friends, whether they work outside the home or not, complain of not having time to do the things that matter to them. Please write down three things you would like to do for yourself next week if you had more time.

1. _____

2. _____

3. _____

We will come back to this activity over the next few days.

# 17
MAY

Look back on yesterday's activity to refresh your memory. How much time would you need to do each activity on your list?

1. _____

2. _____

3. _____

Going back again to your list of three things you would like to do for yourself if you had more time, what is really stopping you from doing your activities?

1. _____

2. _____

3. _____

How could you negotiate to have that time for yourself? How does thinking about this make you feel?

_____

_____

_____

_____

_____

_____

_____

_____

_____

_____

_____

_____

_____

_____

# 18
**MAY**

# 19
MAY

Beginning tomorrow, how could you pick one of the activities on your list and commit to it for the week?

Pick your chosen activity and do it today. If you were not able to carry it out, what prevented you from doing it? How do you feel about this? If you did manage to do it, what did you learn from it?

# 21
## MAY

Explain to anyone who has enabled you to carry out your activity today how they have helped you. Commit to your intention to carry out your activity again tomorrow.

Allowing ourselves time to do what really matters for our health or well-being is an important part of self-love. When others allow you this time, encourage and allow them the same in return.

# 23
## MAY

What did you particularly enjoy about doing your activity? How could you commit to making it a part of your life?

_____

_____

_____

_____

_____

_____

_____

_____

_____

_____

_____

_____

_____

_____

_____

_____

_____

_____

_____

_____

_____

OK, so it's no secret that our bodies and minds have evolved over the years! This weekend, I would like you to think about and jot down what you like and dislike about yourself. Keep it funny! What could you accept and even embrace lovingly? What can you work on?

WE TEND TO READ WHAT WE EXPECT TO (TO) READ.

# Can you find the
# the **mistake**?
# 1 2 3 4 5 6 7 8 9

# Can you find (the) (the) mistake?

1 2 3 4 5 6 7 8 9

What can this illusion teach us? It can teach us that we are quick to form opinions and make decisions and that we feel so sure of our response! Our brain is used to making quick decisions, but we can be wrong quite often. We perceive the world through our filters. We construct our reality. But mindfulness can teach us to come back to our senses again and again, to return to the body and temper our overreactive and hasty belief system so that we may see reality as it really is.

_____

_____

_____

_____

_____

_____

_____

_____

_____

_____

_____

# 26
MAY

Notice how pleasant events can often be mixed with unpleasant emotions (e.g., dreading the end of a pleasant massage). We tend to judge and categorize very fast. When things are pleasant, we want to prolong them or want more. When things are deemed unpleasant, we want to eradicate them as soon as possible. We soon get impatient or frustrated if we cannot change things straight away. Become aware of this process and make some room for discomfort as an opportunity to increase your tolerance and patience. Try noting in the space below a few events that started out pleasantly but became unpleasant. What caused the change? What was your level of tolerance or disappointment?

Think of a best friend. Her qualities. What she would say, be, and do in various situations with you. How she would look at you and hold you when you are down and in trouble. Now be that person to yourself.

*Take-home message*: Be your own best friend. You wouldn't put up with a friend who denigrates you, criticizes you, and hurts you, so don't do that to yourself. Today I caught myself being self-critical when . . . I was my own best friend when . . .

# 28

We usually meditate, or plan to, when we have the time and when we are calm. However, the invitation today is to meditate when you are feeling hot, bothered, irritated, angry, or otherwise perturbed. Difficult emotions are our most profound teachers. The more we can witness our experiences in a nonjudgmental manner, the less suffering we will experience in our lives. If you are not able to meditate in the heat of the emotion, note it down (using adjectives) and try to reconnect with the experience later.

The objective is not to dissect who did what, why, or how but to just stay with the ebb and flow of the moment. Become still, breathe, and allow bodily sensations to arise. Note the emotions (the shortcuts) but connect even more deeply with the physical sensations (pumping temples, clammy hands, butterflies in the tummy, and so on) that tell a deeper truth than does the mind and its memories.

*Mantra for the day*: I am safe. My breath is my anchor. I experience what life and others offer me with kindness and compassion.

Why not stick a recent happy photo here of you smiling or laughing? You don't stop laughing because you are getting old, you get old because you stop laughing!

# 30
MAY

Look at yourself in the mirror! Stick your tongue out! Make silly faces! Fake a laugh! Then go out in the world and make other people laugh!

*Message*: Smiling helps happy hormones to be released, and laughing is a great abdominal exercise. You can always watch a comedy or download some funny podcasts! Being mindful doesn't mean you cannot have fun!

*Blowing hot and cold.* We tend to be quick to complain or try to change our surrounding temperature, as if our body cannot adjust naturally to slight variations. During menopause you may experience hot flashes but also sudden cold spells. If and when you experience temperature changes, notice any physical or emotional reaction to them. Scan your whole body carefully and observe if the change is everywhere or just in certain areas. Investigate its color, shape, texture, how it waxes, and how and when it wanes. Fighting temperature fluctuations or trying to control them will only add to your distress. Allow body temperature changes during menopause to train you to be flexible and tolerant of change and slight discomfort. It can also be a way to reconnect with our bodily sensations and emotions.

# June

She grows more charming with
   the years—
her authenticity appears,
wearing her imperfections
without any corrections.

Her mystery unfolds,
a delight to behold,
the doors that eyes
try to pry,
discovering
inner places.

Exposing her simplicity,
a touch of eccentricity,
her natural colors
adorned with flowers,
a quaint and modest sanctity.

Today, I am really living when . . . Today, I am lost in my thoughts during . . .

### DAWN

Wind in my hair,
breeze on my skin,
the smell of lake water
rinsing away my cares.

A new day is born,
healthy and strong,
life's lungs are infinite,
its heart beats on.

Another offering
bestowed by creation.
A few have tasted the
bitter kiss of death,
and now open the gift
with gratitude.

Do you know what smizing is? It is smiling with your eyes! No mouth, no lips, just the eyes. Keep eye contact with someone whom you'd feel comfortable smiling at. See how the eyes can do the talking. You can also try smizing at the camera and see if you feel a different energy in the moment!

# 3

JUNE

"You should sit in meditation for twenty minutes every day,
unless you're too busy, then you should sit for an hour."
—ZEN PROVERB

What are the obstacles that you have put in place that prevent you from taking time for
yourself?

*Come to your senses.* Do you have 2 minutes right now? Probably, otherwise you wouldn't be reading this. Wake up! Sit down, sit up, and look around. Be totally present to your surroundings. No labeling, no planning. Just be here right now with as much loving-kindness as your heart can muster.

# 5
JUNE

Weather permitting, go outside. Alone or accompanied. Do something you wouldn't usually do. Dare to be daring. Note down what you experienced doing this.

Curiosity is a primary aspect of mindfulness, changing how we pay attention to our experience. When we are curious, we acknowledge what is present with intention and willingness, whether the experience is wanted or unwanted. When a mildly unwanted experience presents itself, notice what happens when you adopt a curious attitude toward it, holding that attitude for as long as you are able. See if you can be curious as well with more progressively difficult or unwanted situations, without exposing yourself to danger.

# 7

JUNE

Menopause has been referred to in English as "the change." In Chinese, the word "change" is the same as the word "crisis." Change or crisis may seem drastic, but if we consider that many wonderful transformations and metamorphoses can arise from changes, we may alter our perspective on a natural change such as menopause. If we cultivate a constant attention that everything (nature, people, objects, relationships, and so on) is always in a state of change, rather than being depressed about the change of life that menopause brings, we may embrace this stage, knowing that it is transitory. Make the most of this interval. What can it bring you today?

Go somewhere quiet. Get comfortable on your cushion or on a chair. Close your eyes. Connect with the sounds around you. See how long you can go in this state. When you are finished, note down what was difficult about your practice today. How is it now?

# 9
## JUNE

Tomorrow we will start a week-long meditation commitment. Plan when your meditation session might best fit in your day and ask other people (colleagues, children, partner) to help you to find this time.

Commit yourself today to a short daily meditative practice for a week. Aim for 15 minutes every day. Today, what thoughts accompany my intention to this practice?

# 11
## JUNE

Today is your first day of 15-minute practice. Plan when and where you will do it. What sensations accompanied my practice?

_____

_____

_____

_____

_____

_____

_____

_____

_____

_____

_____

_____

_____

_____

_____

_____

_____

_____

_____

_____

_____

Do your daily meditative practice. How is this 15-minute meditative practice going? What thoughts come to mind if you manage to stick to it? What is your insight of the day?

# 13

Journal your meditation thoughts for today.

## ONE

It was a bitter divorce—
estranged, her head and body
seemed incompatible
on life's course.

Constantly at war,
as both partners grew up,
but then at fifty, they finally stopped.

They learned to coexist,
ready for the next step
without having to resist.

Head decided:
body had carried her
along as best she could,
executing vital tasks as she stood
in spite of the other's insults and
recriminations since childhood.

Body decided:
head had made the best decisions
to protect her from the vicissitudes
of her existence, in spite of derisions.

They let each other be busy with grace
and agreed to meet often
in the breath space.

They mutually gave up controlling.
They mutually gave up labeling.
They let the other wander in
the field of awareness,
till she'd run out of steam
with fairness.

They welcomed the other,
recognized her qualities
with love and compassion and a
humble apology.

How does meditating daily for 15 minutes make me feel?

# 15
JUNE

What stands in the way of my meditation practice? How do I overcome the obstacles to my meditation practice?

_____

_____

_____

_____

_____

_____

_____

_____

_____

_____

_____

_____

_____

_____

_____

_____

_____

_____

_____

_____

_____

How does meditating help me?
What am I noticing?

# 17

Today look for things that make you feel grateful. Write down five of them at the end of the day. They don't have to be big or important.

1. _____

2. _____

3. _____

4. _____

5. _____

We can be so critical with ourselves and others. Today do this experiment. When you are looking at someone, have benevolent and kind thoughts about them. Look for their individual beauty. Imagine they are someone (a family member or dear friend) whom you really care about. How did this make you feel? How might these thoughts affect your behavior, actions, or posture?

# 19

What do you need to be a meditator? Do you need special skills or attributes? Well, you already have it in you! You were born to love and to feel with another in pain. You don't even need willpower. What you will need is to develop the ability through commitment and practice.

A little puzzle for you. Connect these nine hearts with four straight lines or less without lifting your pen off the paper and not leaving out any or going over any twice.

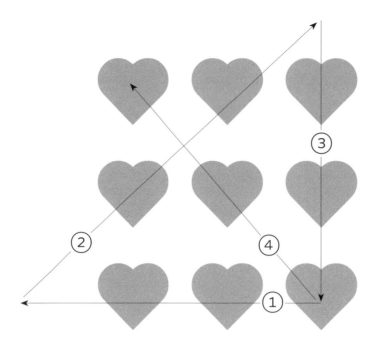

Nobody said the lines can't go beyond the hearts! There are other solutions! This simple exercise shows us that we often limit ourselves in finding a solution by being stuck in our beliefs. Take-home message: think outside the box!

_____

_____

_____

_____

_____

_____

_____

_____

_____

_____

Informal meditation practices today.
Comments?

# 22

JUNE

When meditating, you don't need to force yourself to suppress thoughts, have an empty mind, be totally "thoughtless," or even relaxed. Just let go and accept what comes!

When I am holding on to negative thoughts, I like to imagine an old heavy suitcase that I am carrying around. It is full of things I no longer want. I then say to myself, "Just drop it!" When I agree to do so, I immediately feel light and liberated. Nobody can decide to let go of that heavy burden except me!

Abrupt hormonal fluctuations cause an increase in inflammatory cytokines during menopause. This may be behind the prevalence of cardiovascular disease, osteoporosis, Alzhei-
mer's disease, arthritis, and autoimmune diseases among postmenopausal women. Did you
know that the scientific researcher Dachner Keltner has found that experiencing awe (a
perception of vastness) reduces our inflammatory response (interleukin-6 levels)? Ways
to experience awe could be:

+ listening to music that you love
+ observing nature
+ going to a pet shop or zoo
+ star gazing
+ entering a religious building
+ going to see dinosaur skeletons
+ standing at the foot of a mountain

Try and see if you can make your own list. Maybe put an awesome appointment in your
diary today.

# 24
## JUNE

Dress suitably for the weather where you are, then go outside alone or accompanied and silently watch a fading sunset. Become aware of how colors, clouds, and temperature change. Be aware of any impatience, wanting things to go faster or stay the same.

Do the Body-Scan Meditation. What are you learning about yourself through the Body-Scan Meditation?

# 26

JUNE

Come into any posture. Keep your eyes on one point in front of you and breathe. Experience the soles of your feet, your toes, your spine, any tension in the muscles, the sensation of the air against your skin.

Look out for what stresses you today. How do you experience this stress?

- ☐ physically
- ☐ cognitively (thoughts)
- ☐ affectively (emotions)

How is mindfulness helping you deal with stress differently?

# 28
JUNE

Be aware when stress arises if you feel cut off from your body. Do you feel any of these when you are stressed?

- ☐ numb
- ☐ stuck
- ☐ blocked
- ☐ pins and needles

The mindful approach to dealing with emotions is to neither avoid nor indulge them. Be present to them. A specific tool you can use to deal with emotions is remembering the acronym RAIN.

1. **R**ECOGNIZE: Notice what is coming up emotionally. Give it a label. For example, Anne speaks with her friend on the phone. After the conversation she realizes she feels very irritated. Instead of ignoring or avoiding her discomfort, she looks more closely. She says to herself, "This feels like irritation."
2. **A**CKNOWLEDGE: Accept and allow.
3. **I**NVESTIGATE without getting involved. What are you feeling in your body during the emotion?
4. **N**ONIDENTIFICATION: Can you make the emotion more impersonal? Can you make it the emotion instead of "my emotion"?*

*Adapted from Brach, *True Refuge.*

# 30
## JUNE

This week, let's explore stress further. When faced with acute threat, humans, like other animals, have three potential responses that may be triggered automatically: fight, flight, or freeze. The response is set in motion by a message from the brain (set off through our senses) that causes a discharge of the sympathetic nervous system. Hormones like cortisol and adrenaline are released that have various effects on the body:

- heart rate increases
- blood pressure increases
- blood sugar increases
- the peripheral arteries constrict
- the deep arteries dilate
- breathing rate increases
- digestion decreases
- sweating increases
- pupils dilate
- immune system decreases
- urine production slows or stops
- sleep is prevented
- muscles tense so that one is ready to bolt
- the frontal lobes shut down to increase the speed of response (reacting, not thinking)

These responses allow a burst of energy to muscles to help you get away from the threat, put up a good fight, or freeze (being "scared stiff"). The problem is when the sympathetic system gets triggered in a chronic manner through our modern-day stressors (being stuck in traffic or a stressful day at work), whether these threats are real or imaginary. After the threat is over, it takes between 20 to 60 minutes for the body to return to its pre-arousal levels. This chronic hyperactivation can lead to weight gain (belly fat), diabetes, and heart disease. During menopause, the hormonal changes shown in Figure 1 can make women susceptible to reactions that resemble panic attacks when faced with stressful life events.

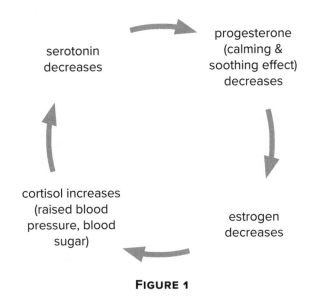

**FIGURE 1**

How mindfulness and yoga can help:

1. One-minute awareness of breath in the moment.
2. Longer meditations after the event.
3. Exercise (light and relaxing). Check out the postures (asanas) for stress.
4. Dealing with thought patterns that set up imaginary catastrophic scenarios and results.
5. Learning to respond rather than react.
6. Breathing in through the nose and a longer exhalation through the mouth.
7. Relaxing poses (e.g., legs up against the wall).

From now on bring close and caring attention to your automatic habitual stress reactions.

# July

There is a place I love to go,
I walk there when I can,
the path meanders up a hill
and looks upon the land.

On the left are luscious paddocks
where horses feed and frolic,
on the right there rolls a dale
where mossy oaks prevail.

The dale divided by a brook
where pebbles bathe and drain,
in mountain water crystal clear
and sometimes topped with rain.

There's something very special there,
perhaps the shades of green,
a perfect natural habitat—
familiar Savanna-like scene.

Each day a changing palette there
with which to feed the senses,
and when I look for refuge there
I drop all my defences.

As you wend your way up high,
the land is farmed for wine,
with nobbled knees
and gnarly hands, the plants
are kept in line.

Continuing from the vines,
the land ascends a peak,
and from that viewpoint,
high above, a vista can you seek.

Like an amphitheater,
the snow-capped mountains at the back,
and next tier is the lake,

in center stage
the fields unfold,
and in the sun they bake.

On one fine day in summer,
when the fields had turned to gold,
I went to Mother Nature
and let my heart unfold.

"I'm entering a new chapter now,
between two halves of life,
I'm more than just a woman, a frau,
a symbol, and a wife."

As She lay there, shorn and bare,
She listened, all ears—
the cricket came with folded hands
and offered me Her prayers.
I bid farewell and off I went,
awakened and aware.

The breeze caressed and blessed my skin,
at peace within, with trust.
With faith, I do entrust,
this season now begins.

Alison was on social media when she saw a photo of her friend in a bikini on holiday. "She has it all," she says to herself, feeling unattractive, unwanted, and alone. Later, while getting ready for bed, she looks at herself in the mirror and notices the lines on her face and her dry, graying hair. She feels angry at the thought of her failed marriage and goes to eat some leftover cake in the kitchen. Afterward she feels even worse and tells herself that she is not only old but also increasingly overweight.

Can you remember times today when an event set off a cascade of thoughts, emotions, and behaviors? If you find it hard to remember, tomorrow set a reminder on your phone or computer and check in on any self-defeating cycles when the alarm sounds.

*You are more than halfway through the year. How are your practice and reflections going so far? What are you learning? How are you engaging with commitment to the entries in the journal? Learning is nonlinear. Each day is a new opportunity to start afresh.*

# 2

JULY

Did you notice any self-critical patterns today? If you did, don't beat yourself up about it. Just note them down.

Ways to handle self-criticism and to increase self-compassion:

+ awareness-of-breath meditation (the Three-Minute Breathing Space or the Five-Minute Mindful Breathing Meditation)
+ focusing on something neutral or pleasant
+ becoming aware of the pattern without feeling the need to fight or ignore it
+ looking at a photo of when you were a child

208

Observe your reactions to three stressful events this week.

Event: _____

Emotion: _____

Reaction: _____

Event: _____

Emotion: _____

Reaction: _____

Event: _____

Emotion: _____

Reaction: _____

Does there appear to be a pattern?

_____

_____

_____

_____

_____

_____

_____

_____

_____

# 4
JULY

Do a meditation.
What are your observations?

_____

_____

_____

_____

_____

_____

_____

_____

_____

_____

_____

_____

_____

_____

_____

_____

_____

_____

_____

_____

_____

_____

_____

Every day people touch our lives near and far. Is there somebody who I would like to thank today? What is stopping me from thanking that special person?

# 6

Bring awareness to your reactions today. Explore the possibility of responding more mindfully. If you feel your reactions are too intense, coming back to the breath will allow you to take some time and distance and make choices more consciously. Remarks?

As we live longer, we will inevitably experience losing people or animals we care about. How can we use this interlude between the chapters of our life to take stock of love and the reality of loss with wisdom, compassion, and an open heart? The following poem is about grief. It's about the passing of a dog, but it could be for any creature. Journal your thoughts on what this poem evokes in you.

LOVE AND LOSS

How do we measure love
when we have loved and lost?
Is there a measure, a unit or a tool,
for something so full of beauty
and yet so very painful?

Is it the species?
Does one love one animal more
    than another?
Is a horse more lovable than a dog?
A cat more than a pig?
Can one love a bird
who comes just to us
to sing their song?

Is it the size of the animal?
Does one love a chihuahua
less than a Great Dane?
Size does not love restrain.
One can love a mouse who
comes to us each day
and looks us in the eye,
her pink cupped paws
her love to us displays.

Or is it the contact and intimacy?
If we carry our dog,

do we love it more than if
the dog gives us his quiet proximity?

Must we matter to the other
for our heart to unfurl?
If we are barricaded,
how can love penetrate?

In love there is a secret,
a secret that is shared.
They've pierced through your
    defences
and visited your soul.
It's like they've scanned your code
and know you in a second.

Is love about protection?
Does the other have to
look out for you,
or can it be one way?
To not love a child who is
    defenseless,
that would certainly be senseless.

Is love about success?
Do we love one who's accomplished
more than we love a tramp?

▶

213

When a tramp is willing to share his only
    meal,
does the tramp's love not appeal?

And when the creature's come and passed,
and grief comes to seize our heart
with its searing, clutching claws,
our pain will manifest
the love that is confessed.

Menopause and gratitude. You may have read that twice, as if those two words don't actually belong together! But every day we can be grateful not just for what we receive but for what we might have and didn't—for all the close calls and missed calamities. What close calls can I be grateful I avoided today? What might you be grateful for from menopause?

# 9
## JULY

This week we are discussing a relevant topic in mindfulness that can be applied to women going through menopause—compassion. Compassion comes from the Latin *cum patior*, to suffer with. Self-compassion, or being kind to oneself, can be an antidote to feelings of worthlessness, or our sense of lack or not being good enough, something women may be experiencing during menopause as the signs of physical and intellectual aging appear. Catch these thoughts the next time you want to denigrate, insult, or belittle yourself and write them down.

*Sarah spills her coffee on her newly laundered work suit as she goes into a meeting. Instead of calling herself an idiot, she rationalizes that she had too many objects to carry and she can cut herself some slack.*

Next time try giving yourself gentle messages and see what thoughts arise in you. For example, do you feel you are too indulgent if you let yourself off the hook?

Did you know that meditation and yoga produce:

+ decreases in blood pressure
+ decreases in muscle tension
+ reductions in insomnia
+ reductions in psychological symptomatology
+ enhanced coping
+ improvements in subjective and objective anxiety and panic[*]

Can you try touching your toes slowly and gently as you let the breath out, extending out into the stretch for 5 seconds, then coming back up on an inhale? Do between five and ten of these.

_____

_____

_____

_____

_____

_____

_____

_____

_____

_____

_____

[*]Park and Han, "Blood Pressure Response to Meditation and Yoga."

# 11
JULY

Studies show that women with high self-compassion experience less interference from hot flashes in daily life. Self-compassion may provide a psychological resource to help women deal with the challenge through self-kindness, a sense of common humanity, and mindfulness. Women low on self-compassion, on the other hand, may worsen hot-flash discomfort through self-criticism.

*Sally experiences a hot flash and feels alone: "I am the only one suffering from hot flashes." And she overidentifies with them: "I am hot and sweaty." These maladaptive reactions, in turn, exacerbate the degree to which symptoms interfere with her life. She then tells herself that she is stupid for feeling this way.*

Think back on your day. When did you practice self-compassion? When did your inner critical voice get in the way?

Everything is temporary. Anything that has a beginning will eventually come to an end. Reality includes mortality, making life precious and unique. Reality is forever changing, always new, whether it is familiar or unfamiliar. Some people never notice the nuance of each experience and repeat the same patterns. Each moment has its beauty, its uniqueness that springs to life and will never recur in the same way. Seize each instant.

Jot down what you notice now in your thoughts. Jot down what you can observe if you close your eyes and reconnect with your bodily sensations.

_____

_____

_____

Color in the mandala mindfully, noticing thoughts, sights, sounds, and bodily sensations that are present.

# 13

Kate (fifty-six years old) has read about mindfulness and self-compassion and has even taken part in an eight-week mindfulness-based stress reduction (MBSR) course but still finds that she is highly self-critical. At times she has night sweats, then becomes anxious and suddenly remembers something she forgot to do at work. Lately she has started asking herself why she is so absentminded and thoughtless.

When certain emotions or repetitive thoughts occur, try investigation, looking at what is behind the experience. In this example, Kate can gently ask, "What is this?" She realizes that at the heart of her problem is her fear of failure. By recognizing this fear of failure and accepting that she has done her best to do her job well, Kate is able to calm her breathing and feel the nervousness in her body dissipate.

What emotion or recurrent thought from your own life would you be interested in exploring here?

Before menopause, many women care and nurture their offspring, often sacrificing their own sleep and rest. As estrogen and oxytocin levels go down, the brain circuits for caring and nurturing go down as well (although they can be reignited by caring for grandchildren or adopting young children). This might be a time to mindfully allow yourself to tell those around you that you are at times unavailable.

How might you communicate that you are unavailable to your work colleagues, family members, or friends? What thoughts or emotions come up when you imagine doing this?

# 15
## JULY

Did you know that 65 percent of divorces are initiated by women during menopause?* One of the regrets many women feel is not having stood up for themselves in their marriage. This is not an invitation for conflict but to be aware of what makes you unhappy in your partner's behavior and being able to communicate this kindly but affirmatively. What are three things that make me unhappy in my relationship?

1. _____

2. _____

3. _____

How could I gently communicate this to my companion and be instrumental in improving the situation?

_____

_____

_____

_____

_____

_____

_____

_____

_____

_____

_____

_____

_____

*Berkson, *Safe Hormones, Smart Women*.

*Menopause, muscle, and joint pain.* Falling estrogen levels can make joints inflamed, stiff, and creaky. Other body changes (e.g., breast size, osteoporosis) can impact posture. Set a timer to ring every hour. Let this be your hourly reminder to check your posture. Verify your weak spots, perhaps poor spine alignment, hunched shoulders, tensed hands. Is your weight evenly distributed? What about your legs and feet? With full awareness, realign your position as best you can. Also let this hourly alarm remind you to drink water, as a hydrated body means hydrated joints.

Journal in the space below: Today's exercise made me . . .

# 17

When you wake up today, open the curtains, shutters, windows. Thank life, your God, the universe for another beautiful day. The weather doesn't matter! What are your observations?

Here is a list of common values:

_____ Authenticity

_____ Autonomy

_____ Courage

_____ Creativity

_____ Fairness

_____ Happiness

_____ Humor

_____ Kindness

_____ Loyalty

_____ Passion

_____ Peace

_____ Respect

_____ Spirituality

_____ Stability

Can you check your top three values or write some of your own in the space below? How have your values changed over the years? Can you think of one way you lived in accordance to your values today and one way that went against them?

_____

_____

_____

_____

_____

_____

_____

_____

_____

# 19

Farming is about carefully picking and sowing the right seeds, cultivating them in the right conditions, and harvesting them at the right moment. In the same way, we must be picky with our time, friends, food, and energy in order to harvest the benefits of a serene menopause.

Today upon waking, pull back the curtains or shutters, open the windows, and give thanks for a beautiful day, whether it's pouring rain or the sun is shining. Now you may be thinking, we already did this! Yes, indeed we did. But every day, every experience is a new opportunity to be grateful. Embrace each experience with fresh eyes and gratitude for that very moment.

# 21
JULY

*Receiving a compliment, gift, or favor.* If this happens today, bring a mindful awareness to feelings of delight or discomfort. How are you breathing? What is your body language? How do you think your answer echoes back to the giver? "Receiving occurs as we simply learn how to be free, free of trying to control and manipulate ourselves or others into being ideal people. A lovely flow of giving and receiving happens naturally as we empty ourselves of rigid expectations, pretense, and judgments"*

*Amodeo, *Dancing with Fire*, 107.

Let's talk about the "L" word! Love is a momentary mind and body state caused by a positive emotion, causing a change of consciousness that expands our sense of self and our surroundings. An experience of oneness and connection is sensed. Today see if you can share a loving moment or more with those close to you, but also with perfect strangers. A smile, a kind word, a shared joke, or just a warmly expressed "Have a nice day!" may be the highlight of someone else's day.

## DHEA: DOSE OF HUMOR EVERY AFTERNOON

They said,
"Mam,
the best thing is yam."
"No," says the boy,
"it's definitely soy."
But I brood
as my mood
turns to food.
The doctor says HRT—
it's the best thing for me.
I'm lost in the pharmacy—
the menopause fairy,
she came and stole my dignity.
My memory's not what
it used to be,
and now there's anxiety.
Sometimes I'm simply angry.

I need 200 calories less, apparently,
than when I was thirty,
but I'm always hungry!
I calm myself down,
I breathe, I smile, I release the frown.
I'm not a hysteric,
I'm simply climacteric!
This is a transition,
so I'll make it my mission
to start with some compassion.
Instead of aggravation,
I'll try some meditation.
So when you think you're going bananas,
'cause it's hot as a savanna,
just get on your mat
and try some asanas.

What moments of fun and humor can I find in my day today?

_____

_____

_____

_____

_____

_____

_____

As we get older and, we hope, wiser, we usually come to believe that using swear words is unacceptable. But what about other forms of bad-mouthing? Today check your negativity as it is conveyed in speech. Make a promise to yourself not to backstab, criticize, or be negative in your words. Be aware of how you say things, and your body language too! Today I stopped myself having a dirty mouth three times:

1. _____

_____

2. _____

_____

3. _____

_____

# 25
## JULY

*Simplicity.* Today try to do something in a very simple way; it could be a meal, how you dress, how you reach a decision. How does this feel? What do I gain by doing this gesture simply? What do I lose by doing it simply?

Women around the time of menopause tend to be the main caregiver of aging parents. Many work and look after children living with them or grandchildren. This adds to the pressures and stresses of life. How can I let off steam today if this is my case? How did I practice self-care (not to be mistaken with self-indulgence!) today?

Write three things you are grateful for today in the empty center of the mandala.

# 27
JULY

"When you are intimate, you are one with. When you are not intimate,
 you are in your head."
—AITKEN ROSHI[*]

What do I associate with the word "intimacy"? Have I felt intimately connected with somebody lately? What desires do I have for intimacy?

_____

_____

_____

_____

_____

_____

_____

_____

_____

_____

_____

_____

_____

_____

_____

_____

_____

_____

[*]In Amodeo, *Dancing with Fire*, 32.

*Partner intimacy*. When you have quiet time together with your partner, sit on the floor or on chairs facing each other, close enough to be able to touch. Set an alarm for 3 minutes. Hold each other's hands in a relaxed way. Look into each other's eyes for the 3 minutes, without talking. What are your comments on this exercise? What are your partner's comments on this exercise?

If you live alone, do this exercise with a mirror. Pay attention to any critical voices and messages.

# 29
JULY

How has mindfulness changed my relationships with friends? With family members? With my partner?

"It is a trillion-dollar industry that would collapse if we believed we were beautiful enough already."

—RUPI KAUR, *The Sun and Her Flowers*

What am I lacking in order to feel that I am good enough as I am?

## 31

JULY

Am I present for my partner for kissing, touching, cuddling, and other forms of intimacy?
If not, what are the obstacles? Could I talk about this with him or her?

### THE FIFTIES

The age of benevolence,
your pistil has blossomed and waned,
your petals are finer,
but you're a warrior.

The curtain goes up,
let the show begin,
your voice is deeper,
no need to weep her.

You used to be headstrong,
your bones are maybe smaller,
but your shoulders are stronger,
trepidation no longer.

Stagnation or generativity,
what will be your legacy?
Will you bring meaning to life?
Does that mean being a wife?
Do not mourn the spirit of youth,
for it is there in truth,

live those unlived dreams,
swim against the stream.

Fill your cup with love,
let it overflow,
set out on a journey
with nowhere fixed to go.

Smile, laugh,
let your tears flow,
chuckle till your teeth show
let your eyes wrinkle,
in that heart there's a twinkle.

Grateful for what you have,
it is enough,
throw away the small stuff.
Love your body,
take a bow,
in age you have the know-how.

# August

If there might be a place on earth
where paradise exists,
the sight I saw upon that day
would certainly contest.

Gleaming cobalt, peacock-blue,
    and aquamarine,
the turquoise waters, crystal clear,
invited me to swim.

Volcanic rock like chocolate cakes,
a quiet bay had formed,
the weathered surface of the
stone was shaped by callous storms.

A billion sprinkled diamonds
on the ripples shone,
and dolphins came to visit me
and in the air had flown.

A turtle swiftly paddled by,
heavy with her home.
A century or two of
living land and sea
and others had survived.

# 1

Time to vacuum! This is a yoga technique that is especially well suited for women going through menopause. As abdominal muscles lose their strength, especially after having children, and due to bad posture caused by sitting for long periods in front of computers, the back muscles get tighter (the lumbar region in the back and the hamstrings at the back of the thigh), and we tend to hunch over more with a rounder, shorter back. This puts additional pressure on the abdominal muscles and the perineum (the area between the anus and vagina), pushing the abdominal organs outward and downward. The following exercise is so great because it really strengthens the transverse muscle that goes around your waist like a belt—consider it the Spanx of your abdominal muscles, if you like! As you do this exercise more and more you will get a tighter tummy as well as more sexual pleasure and better urinary control. Backaches will also improve! The vacuum exercise is to be performed mindfully as much as you can. Doing it in bed before sleep or at the end of a yoga session will also bring deep relaxation.

So let's do it! Breathe in. Breathe slowly out of your mouth while bringing in your tummy as much as possible toward your spine. Imagine squeezing into a tight pair of jeans and sucking your tummy in to show the ribs! You can breathe lightly while holding your tummy in for 20 seconds. Then slowly breathe out and release the contraction. You can also hold your breath out for 3 to 5 seconds before beginning the next round.

You can do the vacuum exercise standing, sitting, lying down, or on all fours. Next time you are getting hot and bothered while stuck in a queue or in traffic, you can do this exercise and feel the difference.

Wounded bird am I.
A voice with loving kindness—
road to peace.
My wings unfurl.

What small action can I take today for self-care?

## 3

AUGUST

*How is my day?* Do you want tomorrow to be a good day? Our happiness should not be conditional to our circumstances. So if we want to have a good day every day, we need to stop outsourcing our happiness and unhappiness to other people or situations. We also have to stop blaming others for our unhappiness!* Today, how did I create my own happiness?

_____

_____

_____

_____

_____

_____

_____

_____

_____

_____

_____

_____

_____

_____

_____

_____

242

*See Kelsang Nyema, "Happiness Is All in Your Mind."

Happiness and unhappiness are states of mind, and therefore their real causes cannot be found outside of the mind. How can we cultivate an internal state of mind? Through meditation. Meditation is a mental action of concentrating on a peaceful, positive state of mind.

*Pose of the day*: Goddess Pose
*Message*: You are in charge of your happiness!

Stand with feet about 3 feet apart and parallel. Rotate the toes outward at 11:00 on the left and 1:00 on the right. Knees and toes should point in the same direction. Bend at the knees and squat downward. Open the arms out, palms up and fingers in gyan mudra (thumb and index finger on both arms touch to form a circle). Heart center is wide open.

# 5

Do you compare yourself with others or even with your younger self? Menopause can be time to take stock and redefine your values of beauty instead of blindly following what the media dictates. What makes you feel beautiful?

*In one of her therapy sessions, Ruby stated, "I have come to the conclusion that my uniqueness is not defined by youth."*

*As for Lara, she proudly declared, "The menopause, like a rite of passage, has allowed me to discover what makes me feel good and to honor myself by doing things that make me feel clean, vibrant, and cared for . . . getting a professional pedicure or massage, for example. Far from self-gratification, I see it more as self-awareness."*

Take a few moments to watch the sunset or just gaze at the sky. Every evening is an opportunity to marvel at the wonders of life. What are your observations today at sunset?

AUGUST

"Your task is not to seek love, but merely to seek and find all the barriers within yourself that you have built against it."

—Schucman and Thetford, *A Course in Miracles*

Menopause is an opportunity for women to unite regardless of race, religion, education, or social standing, thus transcending inequality, racism, and competitiveness. However, as each woman will experience menopause differently, it can also teach us that unity doesn't mean aversion to difference. We are all unique in our difference and different in our uniqueness.

Today reflect on and contemplate your interconnectedness and relationships with other women near and far. You may affect and be affected by many women today, some of whom you will never meet; perhaps they have helped provide you with the food you eat or the clothes you wear, or vice versa. Your life may have been improved or may depend on many ancestral women. You exist in multiple relationships with other women. Practicing mindfulness and contemplating this interconnectedness with other women can help engender a greater insight and realization of how your actions affect other women. It can also awaken a greater appreciation for the present moment you are experiencing and all that is needed to allow that moment to arise.

Animals are so much less inhibited than humans and have far fewer self-imposed rules. Why not take a page out of their book and experiment with doing things differently: get your feet wet even if it's so much colder than the temperature you are used to, splash around, let yourself live the precious, delightful moment! Today I let my hair down and lived the moment by . . .

What comfortable and pleasant or uncomfortable and unpleasant bodily sensations do I notice today? How do I become aware of them? What are my thoughts and reactions to them?

"The grand essentials to happiness in this life are something to do, something to love, and something to hope for."

—GEORGE WASHINGTON BURNAP, *The Sphere and Duties of Woman*

What did you do today? How did you feel doing it? Whom did you show love to today? What are you looking forward to?

# 11
## AUGUST

Today, turn off a habit for a couple of minutes. If you are going to turn on the television, participate in a social activity instead. If you usually take the elevator, take the stairs instead. Rather than use public transportation, try walking, at least the distance of a stop or two. Observe the thoughts that come up when doing this.

## "The Old Man Who Lost His Horse," a Chinese Folk Story

During the Han dynasty (third century BCE) there was a kind old man who lived on the plains outside the Great Wall of China. The gentle old man had only two passions in his life: his son, whom he loved more than anything else, and collecting rare breeds of horses. The old man and his son rode their horses every day. They traveled great distances to trade horses, meet new people, and enjoy the good fortune that life had bestowed upon them. One morning, a servant left the stable door open and one of the old man's favorite stallions escaped. When the neighbors heard the news, they came to comfort the old man, telling him they were sorry he had had such bad luck. But strangely enough, the gentle old man was not upset. He explained to his neighbors that losing the horse wasn't necessarily bad luck. There was no way to predict that the horse would escape, it just happened, and now there was nothing that could be done about it. "There is no reason to be upset," said the old man. The neighbors soon realized that there was nothing they could do to help get the horse back, and that they shouldn't feel sad for the old man's misfortune.

One week later, the stallion came back, bringing with him a mare. This was not just any mare but a rare and valuable white mare. When the neighbors heard of the old man's good luck, they quickly came to congratulate him. But again, the old man was not excited. As he had explained before, it was not necessarily good luck that had brought him this new and beautiful white horse. It just happened, and there was no reason to get excited over it. Still a bit puzzled, the neighbors left as quickly as they had come.

A short time later, while his son was riding the white horse, she slipped and fell. She landed on the son's leg and broke the leg, so that he would always walk with a limp. Again, the neighbors came to the old man's house to express sympathy for the bad luck that had befallen his son. One of the neighbors suggested that the old man sell the mare before any more bad luck could happen, and others said that he should take his revenge and kill the mare. However, the old man did neither. He explained to the neighbors that they should not feel sorrow for his son nor anger toward the mare. It was purely an accident that could not have been predicted, and there was nothing he or they could do to change it. At this point, the neighbors thought the old man was crazy and decided to leave him alone.

Two years later an enemy force invaded the country and all the old man's neighbors were drafted to defend the country against the attack. Because the old man's son was lame, he did not have to join in the fighting. The war was very bad, and most of the old man's neighbors were killed, but his son was spared because he had been hurt by the white horse two years earlier.

The moral of the story: Very often when an event takes place that everybody thinks is good luck, the end results are disastrous. In the same way, an unlucky event can bring about happiness. Therefore you should not lose your will to continue if an unlucky event happens, nor should you be too overjoyed or feel too self-satisfied because of a lucky event or because something that you desire comes very easily to you.

Conclusions:

+ You never know the final outcome of a situation.
+ Don't be judgmental.
+ Things are never as good or as bad as they seem.

Can you express some of your own conclusions?

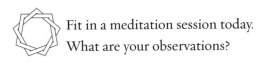 Fit in a meditation session today.
What are your observations?

## MINDFULNESS

Make your intention
to give your attention.
Thoughts are just an invitation—
follow the breath for meditation.
Body and breath,
always in the present.
When your mind is absent,
no need for resentment,
just come back
without being critical.
Even more,
don't be cynical.
Time and again,
it's rather minimal—
make it a habit,
it's a small miracle.

A HAIKU

Must change how it is.
Things are fine the way they are—
just be happy now.

How might the way things are at the moment actually be fine if you don't change them?

_____

_____

_____

_____

_____

_____

_____

_____

_____

_____

_____

_____

_____

_____

_____

_____

"We must not be quick to feel defeated or helpless. Even if an obstacle seems as unyielding as a mountain, we must still find a way through it. In fact, when we look closely, it may be as flimsy as paper."
—*Jing Si Aphorisms*

Today, what mindful thought would you like to examine further?

# 16
AUGUST

Read this slowly and mindfully. Repeat as much as you wish! "I am worthy of love. I don't have to be special, brilliant, or have achieved anything to deserve it. I just need to exist." What feelings or thoughts arise as you say this?

Today notice five sights, four sounds, three sensations, two tastes, and one smell, and journal your observations.

I. _____

_____

_____

2. _____

_____

_____

3. _____

_____

_____

4. _____

_____

_____

5. _____

_____

_____

# 18
## AUGUST

"Be happy in the moment. That's enough."
—MOTHER TERESA

Take some time to watch the sun set tonight. If it is a good night, lie down under the stars and wonder at the infinite space. When you get back, write down something about this experience.

Today, stop eating before you are full. Save the rest for later, share it, or serve less before starting. Perhaps start with serving a spoonful less! This exercise made me feel . . .

# 20

AUGUST

Be there. Be curious. Address life with all the energy you can muster!

Menopause might be an end to our reproductive years, but in many ways it can be a new wind that propels our productive years. In fact, the renowned anthropologist Margaret Mead spoke of the "zest of the postmenopausal woman."* As estrogen declines (even with HRT), and the effect of testosterone (the male hormone) has more influence in our bodies, women can become more irritable, but also more assertive!

Consider which of the following might allow you a new lease of creativity thanks to menopause:

+ No need to worry about pregnancy, periods, contraception.
+ The children are grown/more independent.
+ Sexual satisfaction (my own or my partner's) no longer needs to be my priority.
+ I have more financial security.
+ I have more professional experience.
+ I have more life experience.
+ I no longer need to be a "babe" and can be taken more seriously.
+ Nowadays, women can re-create themselves and their careers at any age.
+ I don't have to do things to please my parents.
+ I have more motivation and gumption.
+ If I pursue studies now it is because I know what interests me and not to prove anything to anyone.

Can you create some of your own observations?

_____

_____

_____

_____

_____

_____

_____

_____

*Lutkehaus, *Margaret Mead.*

# 22
## AUGUST

*Anna has come to realize that since going into menopause she has grown socially distant. After her Body-Scan Meditation, she sets her intention for the day to be more open toward people by saying to herself, "community."*

Before starting the day, set your own personal intention for the day. The intention can be a quality you would like to work on. It is not a goal and you should not attach an expectation to it. It's not the destination but the road map! Write it down in the space below. It can be as simple as to be present.

Before meditating, remind yourself of your intention. Before going to sleep, reflect on how setting this intention and coming back to it created outcomes during your day.

Be aware of what is happening right now. Close your eyes for 1 minute and note the sounds around you.

# 24
AUGUST

Open your eyes to the magic around you today. Note as many occurrences as you can. Try to get to ten observations.

1. _____
_____

2. _____
_____

3. _____
_____

4. _____
_____

5. _____
_____

6. _____
_____

7. _____
_____

8. _____
_____

9. _____
_____

10. _____
_____

Let your body, your age, your situation be a path to your mindfulness practice. As I get older, I am better at . . .

_____

_____

_____

_____

_____

_____

_____

_____

_____

_____

_____

_____

_____

_____

_____

_____

_____

# 26

Invite someone close to you to do a meditation. Afterward, be extra mindful of how you communicate about this experience. Be sure to echo back to the person what their experience was first.

What does spirituality mean for you at this point of your life? Are you working on nourishing your spirituality?

# 28
AUGUST

When I practice mindfulness, it makes going through menopause . . . *Change is a chance for growth.*

"It takes courage to grow up and become who you really are."
—E. E. Cummings

What words come to mind as I dwell on this quote?

# 30

## A Haiku

Her blood is lava.
Eyes closed, she sits with her breath.
All calm now.

*Never stop learning. Never stop doing what you love.* Is there anything you have always wanted to learn? How could learning a new skill, language, sport, or hobby benefit you and others? What is stopping you? If we are patient and committed, we can eventually learn and master almost anything. What could you start with today?

# September

They met in secret at sunset,
their swaying skirts
hiding social stigma and shame.

They came to exchange stories
of their sorrows and their pains,
to take stock and make peace with
nature,
the divine, and with themselves.

They coalesced to mark
the closure of childbirth.
They came to bid farewell
to cycles with the moon.

They came to dance to music,
to howl, to cry, to sing,
to bare their hearts and bosoms,
and let their bodies swing.

They came to burn the taboos
in fires in the sand,
the myths, the attributions,
and all the social views.

The elder, wiser lady
emboldened them to speak,
to take it out of the closet
and honor their physiques.

And so this rite of passage
soon became a practice,
completeness and connection,
and female resurrection.

# 1

*Better than botox.* Becoming conscious of facial lines and wrinkles during menopause leads many women to consider anti-aging injections and surgery to halt the signs of time. However, the exercise this week is risk-free and will make you genuinely more attractive and youthful . . . with no side effects!* The task is to become conscious of your facial expression (you can check in a mirror or take selfies) and make an effort to smile more. Pay attention to how it feels physically: any muscle tension or relaxation in the forehead, the eyelids, the cheeks, the jaw, the lips, the tongue, even how your top and bottom teeth connect. Then zoom in on what's going on in your thoughts as you smile. Is there resistance? Experiment with different types of smiles. Try them all according to the situation. It doesn't have to be a big ear-to-ear smile, just appropriate and genuine.† Smiling has physiological and psychological benefits when you are stressed.‡ In one experiment, smiling participants had lower heart rates during stress recovery than non-smilers, and less of a decrease in positive emotions during a stressful task than did the neutral group.

*Suzanna felt silly doing the smiling exercise. She imagined people would find her strange, perhaps men would get the wrong idea. She realized that in fact her usual expression was not very approachable and that people were much friendlier toward her when she smiled. She felt more positive after doing the smiling exercise for a few days and now pays attention when she inadvertently slips into her grumpy face.*

*Golle, Mast, and Lobmaier, "Something to Smile About."
†Helwig et al., "Dynamic Properties of Successful Smiles."
‡Kraft and Pressman, "Grin and Bear It."

Today, I would like to invite you to become mindful of your sleeping environment. Is your bedroom dark and free of technology? Is your bed comfortable? Is your room the right temperature? A cooler bedroom (17°C / 63°F) will help keep hot flashes at bay. What are your observations?

What thoughts come into your mind when you are coloring the mandala? What physical sensations do you feel?

## LETTING GO

Time to move on, it's over,
a life-stage closure.
Let go and embrace
things as they are.

Close the old doors gently,
open ajar the new,
release your hands,
no longer chagrined,
kiss away the feather
carried on the wind.

Abandon years of accumulation,
one unresolved frustration,
and many small expectations.

Discard cracked, rose-colored glasses
and painful relationship impasses.
Let go of being perfect,
hair grow wild, no longer an object.
Giving up the search for pleasure,
wondering do I really measure.
Good-bye beliefs, regrets, and opinions,
marinating in bitter potions.

Farewell contraception and the
dreaded monthly curse,
routines, schedules, busyness.
Anger, hatred, sadness too,
no need for them,
they make me blue.

Tension in the body,
identity, fantasies, and dreams can go,
fears of being a nobody.

Who are you,
now that you no longer are
who you were before?
Commit to less and
not to more.
You really have come far.

Evict the ruminations squatting,
they haven't paid the rent,
demolish the old story built,
the shoulds, the musts, the guilt.

Dispense with doing it all alone,
avoiding the fear of the unknown.
Fling open the windows to life's
     afternoon,
tear up the schedule of life's morning,
let tears flow and no more hoarding.

Let go of each new breath
to make room for the next.
The bird can choose to leave its cage
and revel in the change.

My present thoughts are . . .

*Become aware of your bodily sensations right now.* Today I would like you to do your yoga sequence, but as much as possible with your eyes closed! This is so that you really feel the movement and postures rather than looking at them and judging what they look like. Lose yourself in your breath. Mindful movement is like mental fitness. The more aware we are of our mental patterns, the more we can move in everyday life or do more demanding physical exercise with understanding and respect for our body.

*Become aware of your emotions right now.* If you awaken at night, bring awareness to how you are relating to the experience of being awake. Notice the thoughts, emotions, and physical sensations. Try opening to the experience without wanting to change it. Simply acknowledge how it is.

*Amina really started fretting when her nights became interrupted during menopause. She was never a big sleeper but was feeling sleep-deprived and grumpy lately. Waking up to go to the bathroom or night sweats would add to her frustration. She would watch the hours on her digital clock passing by, dreading having to be fresh faced for her meetings the next day. Since practicing mindfulness, she is letting go of wanting to control things all the time. Instead of trying to fix things, she now uses her periods of wakefulness to check in with herself and let go. She turns her clock around so that she doesn't monitor time spent awake. Paradoxically, she is sleeping better.*

A Haiku

On a wooden bench.
The sun sets in a pink sky.
Happy me.

The following meditation is to relieve stress. Sit comfortably with a straight, tall spine. Place the hands at the heart center. Connect all the fingers of the right hand to the corresponding fingers on the left hand, with the fingers pointing upward. The palms are spaced apart. Look at the tip of the nose with the eyes half closed. Breathe four times a minute: inhale 5 seconds, hold the breath 5 seconds, exhale 5 seconds, hold the breath out 5 seconds. Continue until you feel calm.

Keep a log of your mindful practice today. Check off the activity when done.

| Activity | Practice | Done |
|---|---|---|
| Ex: Meditation | 40-minute body scan | ✓ |
| Ex: Yoga | 10-minute hatha yoga | ✓ |
| Ex: Daily activity | 5-minute shower, mindfully | ✓ |
|  |  |  |
|  |  |  |
|  |  |  |
|  |  |  |
|  |  |  |
|  |  |  |
|  |  |  |
|  |  |  |
|  |  |  |
|  |  |  |
|  |  |  |
|  |  |  |
|  |  |  |

## 10
**SEPTEMBER**

Today's body. Become aware of your body today, recognizing that it is in a constant state of flux. Today's body may not live up to your harsh expectations. Please be compassionate with it. Your body is doing the best it can! The body is always in the present moment even if the mind is often time traveling. My remarks . . .

What could you grow today? It could be seeds, a plant, or a homemade fermented or sprouted food with recognized nutritional value (e.g., apple-cider vinegar, kimchi pickles, sprouted beans, and so on). Watch the magic over the next few days. We are so lucky to be living in an age of easily accessible recipes and shared knowledge. My remarks . . .

## 12

**SEPTEMBER**

Mindfulness in the supermarket! Next time you go shopping, give yourself extra time. Choose vegetables or fruits you don't usually buy. Make sure your choices are in a rainbow of colors. Don't forget the following foods act like estrogen, so they might help keep hormones in balance.

| FOOD GROUP | TYPES |
|---|---|
| Milk | Soy milk |
| Nuts | Linseeds, pumpkin seeds, sunflower seeds |
| Vegetables | Celery, green beans |
| Fruits | Rhubarb |
| Protein substitutes | Tofu, tempeh |

*Hara hachi bu!* This ancient Japanese practice is such an easy way to improve longevity and keep our waistline. It's easy—just stop eating before you are full. Leave the table while still a little hungry. Ideally you should feel 80 percent full. Another way to improve health is to fast intermittently (eating two meals a day with a long period of about sixteen hours after dinner and before the first meal of the next day) or fast two days a week (consuming around 500 calories on the fasting days).

## 14
SEPTEMBER

Can you slow down, can you say no to a demand, close the door, sit down, feel your feet and bones grounded by the support beneath? Close your eyes and hear the sound of your breath coming and going like the call of the ocean far, far away. My remarks . . .

Am I paying enough attention to notice that I am not paying attention? My remarks . . .

## A Second Chance

The hands glide effortlessly,
like a seasoned skater on a frozen lake.
In joy their pace intensifies,
in boredom will they agonize,
as sullen schoolchildren returning
to an angry home
with a heart as heavy as their satchel,
getting ready for the next battle.

Sometimes they cross over each other,
a momentary peck—
impatient long-term partners
at the airport drop-off point.

Each moment, a blink,
lasts a second.
Forever lost,
out of reach,
forever gone.

Ticking, clicking, forever turning,
never still, forever churning,
an artificial heart restlessly
measuring life's intensity.

Each second a wish granted.
Now and then it's gone,
evaporated into oblivion.

I think of my next wish—
over, late, it's missed
before it's even dished.
I take a bow,
this moment's vow,
my wish—
HAPPY NOW.
Time's up,
the clock stops.

What is on my mind right now, in this instant?

Five ways to bring mindfulness to your meals:

1. Say grace and give thanks before you take your first bite. This can be a lovely ritual when you are eating with others or alone. Just be grateful for the chance to eat together, to eat tasty, nourishing foods, or to be able to prepare food or have someone prepare it for you. Take turns to create the prayer, blessing, or thanks for each meal.
2. Chew foods slowly, enjoying how the flavors develop.
3. Smell the fragrances of each food.
4. Close your eyes when tasting each morsel and try to distinguish the individual ingredients.
5. Listen with as much awareness as possible to how each bite affects your sensations of satiety.

My remarks . . .

## 18
SEPTEMBER

Mindfulness is like an emergency kit to be used in any situation. For example, when we are angry, by investigating our own mind we may discover that in fact we are entitled, over-opinionated, selfish, and so on. Deep down, our behaviors and tendencies might not make us feel good about ourselves. It might not be pleasant to face our demons, but in the long run this discovery will save us from deep-rooted suffering. The following tips might help:

- Acknowledge the emotion—that is, ANGER.
- Imagine what the fly on the wall would say.
- Is there a familiar pattern/trigger?
- Breathe out the anger, long and deep, like a dragon.
- Find some healthy entertainment (exercise, a favorite TV show, a cool shower).
- Write a letter, not to send but to vent.
- If the anger is still lingering unresolved and you cannot forgive the person, speak to a professional.

My Inner Garden

I am cultivating my inner garden.
I will kindly dismiss the wardens,
make a path through my busy thoughts,
and line it with children's handmade pots
in which I will plant small seeds of love, laughter, and patience.
Water them daily with loving presence,
give the worries a long vacation,
and be there for friends with dedication.
Wake up early with motivation,
sprout small ripe berries of inspiration,
seasonal trims of expectations,
and enrich the soil with tender sensations.

Choose a sequence of yoga that helps keep you flexible and toned. Practice it as often as you can to see the maximum benefits. At the end, jot down one word that summarizes your experience.

# 20
SEPTEMBER

I hope by now you realize that you don't need to get into any particular position or be in any particular place to meditate, but that any object can be an opportunity to bring gratitude, joy, awe, and connection to you.

What do you wish from your day? For example, you may wish for patience, kindness, focus, or calm. Can you make a small reminder on a sticky note, a screen saver, or even a colorful spot somewhere? What is your word today?

What narratives do I recount about myself? What labels or adjectives do I use to describe myself? How fixed or nuanced are these traits? Beware of using words such as "always," "never," "must," or "should," and allow yourself the freedom to evolve.

# 22

*Mindful to life's cues.* As you wake up in the morning, today or tomorrow, set an intention for guidance and for greater awareness to questions you need answered. For example: "I need answers to my most intimate relationship." "I need pointers in my professional life." "Universe, please give me guidance on how to talk to my angry son." Be open to conversations, songs, newspaper articles, books, and people's expressions and reactions. By opening your eyes and ears you may find new answers. Life often gives us answers, we just have to be open and receptive to them.

Be aware today of your behavior. Are you happy with the way you behaved today in certain situations? What could you do to change the behaviors you are not happy with?

# 24

"When I eat, I eat."

—THICH NHAT HANH, *How to Eat*

Choose a selection of fresh, plant-based ingredients. Some protein is necessary to maintain muscle mass. Make sure you are comfortable and choose your surroundings mindfully. Enjoy eating your meal in silence (no phone, laptop, or reading)! Do nothing other than concentrate on the wonderful taste, textures, and colors of your food.

## SUFFICIENT

I am beautiful enough,
thin enough,
curvy enough.
My hair is thick enough,
long enough,
tame enough.
shiny enough.
My grays are badges of my valor.
I am friendly enough,
reserved enough,
wild enough.
I am smart enough,
clever enough,
humble enough.
My house is cozy enough,
clean enough,
safe enough.
Enough is enough—
I am good enough,
yesterday, today, and tomorrow.

What does this poem evoke in you? How do you handle criticism about your appearance, performance, or personality?

_____

_____

_____

_____

_____

_____

_____

_____

_____

_____

# 26

SEPTEMBER

Do as many yoga postures as you have the time and energy for. What are my observations?

LIMES

I could have ignored them,
not recognized their existence
until I needed them.
They now sit huddled in a bowl
on the dining room table.
I give them my attention,
all eight of them.
Two are darker—
each lime's color upon closer inspection
unfamiliar, eluding final detection,
as the light bounces off its shielding skin
as round and ripe as nubile breasts.
Small pores along their surface come to my awareness
like roughly weathered human flesh,
its pores enlarged by years of sweating.
its bottom looking like a small nipple,
its umbilical cord like a newborn baby's—dry and crusty.
I ponder its magic,
eager to taste its sharp juice.

What are my emotions right now?

_____

_____

_____

_____

_____

_____

_____

# 28
SEPTEMBER

What are my usual reactions to stress? Do I get lost in my thoughts? If so, what are they? Do I get lost in external pursuits? If so, what are they?

What turns me on in my partner:

_____

_____

_____

_____

_____

_____

_____

Will I tell my partner this? If yes, great. If not, what makes it difficult to express myself to him or her?

_____

_____

_____

_____

_____

_____

_____

_____

# 30
SEPTEMBER

"Every man or woman who is sane, every man or woman who has the feeling of being a person in the world, and for whom the world means something, every happy person, is in infinite debt to a woman."
—WINNICOTT, *Winnicott on the Child*

What are your thoughts?

# October

Nobody sees
this furnace deep inside of me—
red, orange, and peach,
it is stoked by passion,
it is forging who I am.
My heart is not cold and hard.
This heat reminds me,
regenerating
from the embers:
I am born again
each day.

# 1

Today try "unitasking"! Do one thing at a time and do it with undivided attention.

Tasks:

1. _____

2. _____

3. _____

4. _____

Do less and do it with all your awareness and attention. What are your observations?

_____

_____

_____

_____

_____

_____

_____

_____

_____

_____

_____

_____

_____

Check in at various points today and assess your levels of energy or depletion:

| LOTS OF ENERGY | DEPLETED |
|---|---|
|  |  |
|  |  |
|  |  |
|  |  |
|  |  |
|  |  |

# 3

*My small wonders today.* Today, take some photos on your phone of the smallest miracles or small wonders that you come across. At the end of the day, look through the photos and write down what they were.

*Creating space in the day for a pause*. This is a 1-minute practice to weave into your day to put some distance in between any stimulus and response:

STOP!

1. **S**top what you are doing.
2. **T**ake an inbreath, take an outbreath, slow and easy.
3. **O**bserve your experience, your thoughts, your emotions.
4. **P**roceed with whatever helps you to continue mindfully and with a smile.

What are some of your observations for today?

Try commenting on your body in a neutral way. Watch yourself for self-critical thoughts today and change your internal message to a neutral one. How might considering our body in a neutral manner help us make peace with it?

Our body is forever evolving. We cannot always be positive about it. However, neutrality may be more achievable than being positive and is more compassionate than berating or criticizing our perceived imperfections. Just like changing gears when driving a stick-shift vehicle, you need to go into neutral when switching from reverse (negativity) into first gear (a more compassionate frame of mind).

Today, as much as possible, try to measure non-essential appointments in terms of rhythms or cycles rather than time. Be conscious of things in your inner and outer world that are determined by natural rhythms rather than chronological time. What are your observations?

## 7

*Right effort.* Today try to find the moments when you try too hard or give up too easily. This can pertain to your body: How much do you push yourself when exercising, or do you stop as soon it starts getting challenging? What about with your work: Do you need to work overtime instead of spending valuable family time? Think of a happy medium when doing an activity from start to finish or at various points during the day. What are your observations?

Be patient with your meditation practice. Small, incremental steps are the way to go. Experiment with different times and places until you find those that can become part of a routine and ritual.

Today, I meditated for about _____ minutes in the <u>morning</u>/<u>afternoon</u>.

My chosen spot was _____.

This <u>fitted in</u>/<u>didn't fit in</u> my regular schedule.

I liked the _____ of today's practice.

I disliked the _____ of today's practice.

_____

_____

_____

_____

_____

_____

_____

_____

_____

_____

_____

_____

_____

# 9

Reflect on your mindfulness journey so far. What are your accomplishments?

Today check in on these questions when you eat. How hungry am I on a scale of 0 to 5?

— 0  — 1  — 2  — 3  — 4  — 5

How do I feel the hunger?

☐  I feel light-headed or dizzy

☐  stomach grumbles

☐  acidity in the stomach

☐  headache

☐  I feel like changing the taste in my mouth

I eat:

☐ fast    ☐ slowly    ☐ one thing at a time    ☐ I tend to do something else while eating

Am I making mealtimes a time to sit down and listen to what my body is telling me? Am I nourishing my body, my mind, my taste buds?

_____

_____

_____

_____

_____

_____

_____

_____

_____

## 11
OCTOBER

What informal mindfulness practices have worked for me today? These could be brushing your hair, washing dishes, sewing, writing an email . . . everything we do can be done mindfully.

My yoga practice today included:

## 13
OCTOBER

*Grasping.* It is necessary to invest in and commit to our friends, family, passions, careers, beliefs, and so on. But when this becomes craving, clinging, grasping, or over-attachment, it can lead to unnecessary suffering. It is the difference between cradling a flower or clinging to a flower and crushing it. Which of these do I cling to?

- ☐ spiritual practice
- ☐ views
- ☐ opinions
- ☐ judgments
- ☐ pleasure
- ☐ stories, interpretations, or narratives
- ☐ objects of desire
- ☐ people

Distraction, negative self-talk, criticism, and self-doubt are detrimental to intimacy with our partner. Catch yourself when you are losing the precious moment to these negative thoughts.

## SUPERWOMAN

Two minutes,
maybe three,
to tell the story of how it's been.

Nine women,
one man.

She talks of her kids,
of how she may fail,
a bittersweet tale
of giving her best
that is never put to rest.

The other speaks of liberation,
storing the wisdom of contemplation,
learning as a preparation.

As for her, she's always running,
pushing, guiding, watching.
She thinks she's indispensable—
maybe she is, but control is reprehensible.

As for me, I'm always learning,
mind always and forever churning,
a work in constant progress,
each day a new line to address.

We want to belong,
be unique and strong,
a force to be tamed,
silencing even the male.

# 15
OCTOBER

Today, think about things you can be grateful for at this moment in your life. Count them on your fingers and see if you can get to ten. Think about this throughout the day, then write them down.

1. _____

_____

2. _____

_____

3. _____

_____

4. _____

_____

5. _____

_____

6. _____

_____

7. _____

_____

8. _____

_____

9. _____

_____

10. _____

_____

How do you spend your time? What do you tend to complain about regarding your time management that has become repetitive or chronic? If you were to find out today that you had five years to live, what would you do differently?

Today I spent most of my day . . .

_____

_____

_____

. . . a part of my day . . .

_____

_____

_____

Thinking of this makes me feel . . .

_____

_____

_____

Tomorrow I might try . . .

_____

_____

_____

# 17

Put down your spanner
and your hammer—
you are not broken,
you do not need to be fixed.
No need for repair,
do not despair.
Perfect in imperfection—
take an honest look,
do not judge,
but dare to be aware,
and ask yourself,
does your life
live up to your values?

Let moments of stress be perfect opportunities to practice checking in with self-compassion to thoughts, sensations, and emotions.

*Helen is on her way to the airport and feels time racing by as her check-in time gets nearer. She takes a deep breath and recognizes that the thoughts are "worry." She checks into her body and realizes that she is hunching her shoulders and has a tummy ache. She scans her emotional temperature and says to herself, "anger." She consciously takes a few deep belly breaths. She allows her shoulders to relax. She recognizes that worrying will not help her get to the airport faster.*

When I am stressed my breath becomes . . .

# 19

Write a short gratitude letter to someone whom you would like to thank in person but never got the chance to.

- ✦ Arrange to meet the person and let them know how grateful you are. Tell them that you would like to read something to them.
- ✦ Read the letter slowly. Notice your emotions and theirs as you read it to them.
- ✦ When you have finished, give them time to digest and give their feedback.
- ✦ Let them keep the letter upon parting.
- ✦ If it is not practical to meet them in person, perhaps arrange a phone call or video call.

The following plan might help guide you:

Dear _____ ,

I wanted you to know how grateful I am to you for

_____ .

When I was _____ ,

you really helped me by _____ .

Today, I am living in _____ . I am _____ and _____ .

Thank you for showing me _____ .

This exercise is very moving. It can help us refocus on the wonderful people who are often forgotten in our lives. It generates happy feelings in both the writer and the receiver of the letter.

_____

_____

_____

_____

_____

What activities do you do that allow you to live in the present? Make a list and see if you can expand it just a little.

# 21
## OCTOBER

Can you do an hour-long meditation? Set your phone to ring in an hour and see how long you can meditate. If you only reach a couple of minutes, check in with yourself and express any words that accompany the exercise. Be compassionate with yourself. The exercise is not to beat yourself up but to become aware.

*Looking at things with fresh eyes today.* Have you ever noticed how children are fascinated by things that adults often ignore? Today, look at things that you take for granted with fresh eyes. Stop to marvel at your environment. Nature is an easy source of awe.

## 23
OCTOBER

TAKE YOUR SHOES OFF

Take your shoes off,
let down your hair,
step on the wet grass
as if you don't care.

Forget all prohibitions—
get your feet wet,
feel the mud trickle
and the ladybird fret.

She said, "You'll get sick,"
and you listened . . . 'til now—
shoes off with a kick,
defiance in your brow.

Sensual, cool,
unleashed to the core,
liberation in the air,
anchored to the floor.

How might you let your inner child find some playful moments today? What might hold
you back?

_____

_____

_____

_____

_____

_____

_____

*Squatting frogs.* Squatting is an exercise that we can do almost anywhere and that has great benefits for the legs, glutes, and sexual organs, as it helps to increase circulation in the pelvic area. You can hold on to the side of a table or put your hands in *Namaste* together at the sternum. Just make sure your knees don't over-project past your feet. Do the repetitions slowly and breathe deeply. Start with two to three sets and try and build how many you can do over time. Caution should be followed by those who have knee issues. First-timers should focus on the breath and on the quality of the movement rather than quantity.

THINK before you speak! Ask yourself:

**T** Is it true?

**H** Is it helpful?

**I** Is it inspiring?

**N** Is it necessary?

**K** Is it kind?

Do you have an example for the day that you can jot down? Even one word will do!

Take a few moments for solitude today. Bring awareness to your belly region and connect with the temperature and any sensations therein.

## SURGICAL MENOPAUSE

The house is no longer a home.
There is still light around,
some warmth on the ground,
perhaps more than afore?
It is not closed, the door.
The home of her first child,
and her second, too.
They took it away
that white day.
Now she bleeds no more,
but she is more of a mother
than she was ever before.
Mother to her child,
and her child's children . . .
no need to chide them,
nothing forbidden,
her heart is open
like a late summer garden.

# 27
OCTOBER

Do a yoga sequence, then jot down your observations.
My expectations today were:

_____

_____

_____

_____

The reality of my practice today was that:

_____

_____

_____

_____

Whether coming to the meditation cushion or your yoga mat, drop your expectations and just come with a curious mind!

_____

_____

_____

_____

_____

_____

_____

_____

Meditation can be frightening and distressing as we tear down the walls of illusion we have built to shield ourselves from reality. Don't avoid the process. Let the thinking run its course and observe it (as fantasy or memory) without getting enrolled in the plot.

# 29

Which of the following obstacles pop up
in my meditation?

- ☐ doubt
- ☐ craving
- ☐ desire
- ☐ fantasy
- ☐ agitation
- ☐ aversion
- ☐ boredom

When they do, I recognize them and move back to the breath.

If you feel bored when meditating, try looking again. Be mindful of the object of your awareness with the eyes, ears, and sense of a child. Investigating boredom. Where is it in my body? What does it feel like? What does it do to my thought processes?

# 31

OCTOBER

I start the day with _____ on my mind. In meditation,
I have good days and bad days. How was mine today? What might be the cause?

# November

If I could choose a quality,
it would be humility.
As strong and grounded
as a tree,
almost living eternally,
in perfect anonymity.

Mindfulness always has some object. Any object or mental state in the here and now can do. You can be mindful of your breathing, mindful of pain, or mindful of an emotion. Whatever your object, be aware of its fluctuation.

Obstacles to meditation can include positive mental states (happiness, compassion, contentment). Recognize that these too are mental states that come and go, without holding on to them.

## 3
NOVEMBER

I wake up with the sensation of _____. What are the first thoughts that enter your mind as you gradually come to consciousness after sleep? How can you slowly hone in on your surroundings and use your senses to appreciate what this new day brings you?

_____

_____

_____

_____

_____

_____

_____

_____

_____

_____

_____

_____

_____

_____

_____

_____

_____

_____

_____

Choose a meditation practice. What difficulties arise? Remember, difficulties are an integral part of your practice and are precious opportunities for learning.

Mindfulness does not take up more time in your day. It may actually end up saving you time. Think of the following and check which one resonates with you today. When I am mindful:

___ I pay more attention and forget less.

___ I do the same things, but the time spent doing them is enriched.

___ I make fewer mistakes.

___ I sleep better at night, and that impacts the following day.

___ I have fewer energy-sapping conflicts with those around me.

Closely tied to non-striving is the ability to trust. How might we apply trust to the experience of menopause?

+ Trust in change taking time and the ability to self-regulate.
+ Trust in getting healthy through good habits.
+ Trust in finding good, quality sleep with proper sleep hygiene.
+ Trusting in oneself through mindful attention during hot flashes, mood swings, or memory lapses.
+ Building trustworthy relationships.
+ Creating a quiet space in your home to practice meditation and yoga.

Care for yourself, look after yourself. It is a great demonstration of love for those you love.

Right now, I make _____ the object of my trust.

# 7

Notice moments today when you feel connected, joyful, expressive, loving, and purposeful. What are you doing when this arises? Who are you with? What are you allowing?

We have limited time and resources (physical energy, mental energy, and earnings) to spend on what nourishes our body, mind, and soul. How will I spend, prioritize, and protect my resources today? What am I willing to forgo?

## ANGER

You pour down me
like melting magma,
fusing my fascia with fury.
You make me tremble with terror
at the intensity of my affect.

I pant, sweating to stay calm,
passion ploughing through my pulse.
My ego eggs me to fight back,
to resist, to repel, and to revenge.

My spirit suffocating for stillness,
for the anger of the storm to subside
as it struggles to survive

I know that deep inside
a choice there does reside
to release or nourish pride,
for guilt or to begrudge,
imprisoned or be free.

I breathe and fist release,
acquitted I can be.

As reproductive hormones wane, unpredictable changes in mood and bodily reactions can leave us experiencing emotions in an intense way. Sometimes there isn't a win-win or lose-lose situation, but choices. What can we let go of to further our path to serenity?

_____

_____

_____

_____

_____

_____

_____

Do the Metta (Loving-Kindness) Meditation (p. 411). What was good about this practice? What was difficult about this practice?

Are you making meditation a regular practice? What could help make it easier for you to turn it into a habit?

# 11

**NOVEMBER**

What is the narrative concerning menopause that you have been handed by your culture, your mother, older female figures, and your social group? Give yourself some time to reflect on these. To what extent are these beliefs conditioned and unquestioned? Are there any fears? How can you question, explore, observe, and reflect on these narratives with open curiosity?

Give thanks to three things this morning:

_____

_____

_____

It is best to plan the length of your meditation session before starting. Don't start to think about time once you begin, as this may make you restless.

_____

_____

_____

_____

_____

_____

_____

_____

_____

_____

_____

_____

_____

### GRACEFUL AGING

My lips will no longer libel
to keep them soft and sweet.
My eyes will no longer scrutinize
to nip those nasty lines.
My skin will soften up
to drink the message cup.
My hand will unfurl
to help, to hold, to heal.
My breast will beat to love,
and not to fear or hate.

My soul will be a crutch
for those who need my strength.
I'll share my food with you,
and that way we'll be two.
We'll toast to keeping slim
'cause splitting keeps you trim.
My wrinkles will lay witness
to wisdom, depth, and fitness.
And for every long, white hair,
my humor will it bare.

Your morning practice will take place as you open your eyes. Upon waking, set your intention for the day using one of these concepts as a springboard.

Patience
Kindness
Compassion
Gratitude
Generosity
Serenity
Joyful
Listener
Beginner's mind

# 15
## NOVEMBER

Today, make patience your intention.

## ODE TO MATURITY

Time to be free—
knowledge is wisdom,
I can be me.

How can I distinguish my ego from my calling? As we go toward menopause and into it, this new life stage with its closure of our biological productivity may make us ponder and assess our accomplishments in life. While Western culture orients us toward performance and attainment, mindfulness encourages us to see ourselves as in communion with the world around us and not so separate! How can mindfulness help us find our true calling at this moment in life and put our pride (ego) aside? Ego thrives on fears and anxiety and helps you maintain a sense of identity. It shows the world who you want to be, ought to be, should be, or must be. Calling thrives on self-reflection, self-knowledge, and self-discovery. It is your authentic and soulful connection with the universe. It shows the world who you *really* are.

Do some yoga today. Feel the movements as you perform slowly. How does your breath affect the movement and the movement affect the breath? Observations:

# 17
## NOVEMBER

Do the Three-Minute Breathing Space meditation (p. 409) today as many times as possible. What are your observations?

"Don't do any task in order to get it over with. Resolve to do each job
in a relaxed way, with all your attention. Enjoy and be one with your work."
—THICH NHAT HANH, *The Miracle of Mindfulness*

Enjoy the process of tasks you usually do absentmindedly, impatiently, or begrudgingly. Try
to do them artfully, lovingly, or delicately, depending on the situation.

*I usually cook dinner at the end of the day in a rush and feeling irritated by my own impatience and fatigue.
Today I took extra time to buy fresh ingredients carefully. I interacted with the sellers (instead of listening to
my music), and I dedicated myself to food prepping for the week. I enjoyed the smells, colors, and textures of the
raw produce. I enjoyed experimenting with two new recipes. I also ended up eating more healthily all week and
saving time and money!*

# 19
NOVEMBER

"Silence is not silent. Silence speaks. It speaks more eloquently.
Silence is not still. Silence leads. It leads most perfectly."
—Sri Chinmoy, "Silence Speaks, Silence Leads"

It is not easy to face our despair during meditation, and when we are feeling good, meditating may seem the last thing we need to do! At times our inner world might seem like a refuge from a cruel outer world. However, we should try to stay connected with the influence of the outer world too. If at other times the outer world might seem to be much more beautiful than the inner darkness within, let the outer world let in a glimmer of light. Mindfulness can be the bridge between our inner reality and the one outside.

You knew me from the start,
the one who made me feel loved,
that very special person who arrived,
looked through my tears
and learned the secrets in my soul
the others didn't know how to read,
or didn't hold the key,
or couldn't speak the language—
perhaps they had too much baggage?
Or were the words written in another tongue?
Maybe they were just too young.
But you have read the music,
played it with the finest notes,
the spark in me you did evoke,
and since that day my story wrote.

What do I feel connected to? What increases my sense of well-being in this present moment?

# 21
## NOVEMBER

*Naikan meditation?* Morita, a great Zen master, proposed that reflecting on these three questions for three days would enable us to move on peacefully in a dispute: *

1. What have I received from the person?
2. What have I given to the person?
3. What problems have I caused the person?

Dwell on these questions throughout the day. At the end of the day, come back and answer them. They can concern big or small things. The smallest often seem so important for our day-to-day survival! The questions can be guided toward any situation, any relationship (with a person, animal, or object), and for any duration of time (over the years, today, a moment). Reflecting on these questions and the answers that arise can help us take responsibility for our actions and make us see the part we play in a situation. We tend to be quick to blame others but cut ourselves a fair amount of slack!

*Adapted from García and Miralles, *Ikigai.*

A thought experiment that I have often played is to ask myself: "Am I a pleasant partner? If I were someone else, would I want to date myself? If I were someone else dating someone just like me, how could I be a more lovable partner?" Small games like this invite us to be mentally flexible, seeing things from other perspectives.

# 23
NOVEMBER

Before you get out of bed, close your eyes, take a few breaths, and just connect to your state of wakefulness. As you go through your day, face whatever situation comes up as an opportunity to write about it using poetry—it's easy and a great way to defuse over-identification. You can try rhyme, metaphors, or alliteration. You may be a poet, . . . but you just don't know it!

## GIGARO

Pine trees flair
like fuzzy short hair
atop a lanky adolescent.
Silhouetted high
on a graduated sky,
an undulating carpet
of a winter sea,
pulling the rug from
its backdrop feet.

The waves growling
from an inward howling.
A billion pebbles tumbling,

wending their way to the shore.
An unrelenting belly
clamoring for more.

Salt mist lining my nose,
a freshly dewed rose.

The sun sinking in slow motion,
a flash of gold potion.

Breeze fanning my skin,
a punkawallah in a trance,
never questioning his chance.

When you are having a difficult moment, are feeling hot, flustered, irritated, or angry, that is the reality. Don't avoid it. Look it in the eye. Examine the experience, observe it mindfully. Learn its modus operandi. A bit of reverse engineering can help you learn how to pull the process apart and dismantle it! What were today's tough moments for me?

# 25

**NOVEMBER**

Together with _____ I have achieved _____.

I feel like a member of a community when:

_____.

Hey honey,
stay with me, don't flee,
even if I may bring you discomfort.
For it is plain to see
that facing some pain
might set you free.
It might help you grow—
what you fear most,
not that which distracts you,
your usual ghost.

Don't get me wrong,
I know you must be strong,
and sometimes deep fragility
seems to be your speciality.

But if you stay with me,
you will get to see
your modus operandi,

how you avoid
intimacy and void.
So dare to take off your mask,
make-up, clothes, and share.
Look at yourself
in the mirror, head to toe—
Who are you really?
Nobody better than you can know.
Please embrace yourself,
give yourself a star,
you've come this far.
Hug yourself, and please do smile,
you've done the miles.
Give yourself love,
and please don't ration it.
Embrace yourself with pure compassion—
if you cease your flagellation,
you'll arrive at a new constellation.

"The essence of our experience is change. Change is incessant.
Moment by moment life flows by, and it is never the same.
Perpetual fluctuation is the essence of the perceptual universe."
—BHANTE GUNARATANA, *Mindfulness in Plain English*

What has changed for you today?

# 27
NOVEMBER

I will be happy if or when . . .

1. _____

2. _____

3. _____

We put our happiness on hold in the mistaken belief that things will be different when we achieve that promotion, weight loss, mortgage, diploma, and so on. Although there are situations that can strengthen our health and safety, unfortunately they are not the things we often put our happiness on hold for.

_____

_____

_____

_____

_____

_____

_____

_____

_____

_____

_____

_____

_____

_____

What activities did I do today that were replenishing, soothing, or nourishing to my soul?

# 29
## NOVEMBER

Which activities drained me of my energy today? Try at least one of the energizing or restorative poses in the yoga section at the back of the book.

Today be aware of when you judge things or even label them as "good," "bad," or "neutral." Notice when you try to shy away from or block what you label as "bad" and grasp, try to prolong, or get more of what you classify as "good." Notice how what you might classify as "neutral" gets little attention.

Good:

_____

Bad:

_____

Neutral:

_____

Now see if you can remember a situation that you judged to be bad but that in the long run turned out not to be so.

_____

_____

_____

_____

_____

_____

_____

_____

_____

_____

# December

Mist wraps the land in
a cloudy cloak of mystery.
I too want to don the robe
and cradle the cool cloth
against my heated breast.
Feeling my spirit soar
like a bucking horse,
and energy expelled,
I return to my essence,
calm and free.
I am one with my surroundings—
osmotic presence,
I smile in peace.

# 1

This is the festive season in many cultures. If you celebrate Hannukah, Ramadan, Diwali, or other holy days, you can use the mindfulness tips in the following pages for the upcoming holiday season.

As women, we are often in charge of decoration, food preparation, and welcoming guests into our homes. This can be challenging in the best of times. Add to this the aches, mood swings, and energy dips of menopause, and we can really get into a sticky situation. So this month I will be focusing on self-care, setting boundaries with others, redefining our values, and being there for others. It's a tall order, I know! But a little preparation (and your journal is here to help you) promises to help make this season one of your most mindful and serene to date. Let's get started.

Journal what emotions arise in you at the thought of Christmas or any other celebrated festival. (You can look at the wheel of emotions on p. 69 if you need inspiration.)

This month buy some cards. For each person of importance in your life, write a heartfelt note. Spend a few minutes every day telling that person why they matter to you. If this is difficult to do, what are some of the reasons?

Do the Goddess Pose.
How long and how steady can you be? Observations:

There are many cultural and archetypal symbols of how women should be and look. Think about this during your day. How does it feel in your body when you are up against these explicit or implicit messages? Scan for any reactivity. How do you tend to judge yourself or others on body weight, fashion, or hairstyle, for example?

## HAIR

She decided to let it be—
give it freedom,
wait and see.

Mark the passage
of time and age,
no more damage,
resistance rage.

Keep a track
down her back,
ripe with memories,
each strand a victory,
unless it bailed out naturally.

Growth rings
of ease, and challenging.
The past tracking,
learning,
growing unrelentlessly—
recounting history
organically.

Each month an inch,
life's cinch,
like fresh white snow.
Cover it with mud,
make it red as blood,

then tone it down
to chestnut brown.

At first it reached the jaw . . .
was there time to touch the floor?
It grew to life,
feminine archetype—
loving wife
Kali, siren, goddess,
Mother Earth, long as grass,
symbol of strength and femininity,
wisdom and beauty,
fragility and insecurity.
Each woman's responsibility
to exile expectations honestly.

Coiled kundalini—
braiding unity with infinity,
weaving past and present, creating now,
or unfettered in free fall.

Extrasensory perception,
and to all things connection,
reaching out like tentacles—
energy receptacle.

A sharp cut to honor grief,
turn over a new leaf.

A respite from the suffering,
a sacrificial offering.
A fresh beginning,
it needed to be done—

let bygones be bygones,
chopping down the past,
and make the present last.

As hair can grow thinner and hair fall increases during menopause, we can take a few minutes of our day to brush our hair mindfully. One exercise I relish every day is to invert my head and brush my hair from the scalp to the ends with my favorite hairbrush. This increases blood flow to the scalp, distributes protective oils from the scalp to the drier ends, and feels heavenly after a stressful day.

_____

_____

_____

_____

_____

_____

_____

_____

_____

_____

_____

_____

# 4

DECEMBER

Carry on with the writing exercise from December 2. What thoughts accompany this exercise? What emotions accompany this exercise?

374

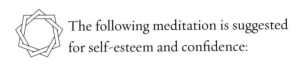 The following meditation is suggested
for self-esteem and confidence:

*The mantra*: "Wise, worthy, and strong, I thrive."

*Posture*: Sit in easy pose.

*Mudra* (hand gesture): The left thumb meets the nail tip of the left pinkie. The middle
  fingers stay straight. You can rest the back of your hands on your thighs.

*Pranayama* (breath): Breathe slow and deep.

*Drishti* (eye gaze): On an object in front of you.

What are your observations?"

# 6

During menopause, some women experience unsettling and unexpected sensations (such as pins and needles, increased sensitivity, burning sensations, or cold hands or feet). This is primarily due to fluctuating estrogen levels on the central nervous system. Some of the following can help:

+ Breathing exercises
+ Mindful walking
+ Mindful water drinking
+ Aiming for eight hours of sleep every night

Which of these did you manage today?

What self-care exercise would I like to find time for today? Once I have done the exercise, how did it make me feel? Why is this self-care exercise important for me?

Today try and connect to your bodily sensations throughout the day. Be conscious of what you are doing, where you are, and what your body, or parts of it, feel. "By living more in our body and welcoming its vibrant (and sometimes uncomfortable) feelings, we become more present to ourselves and, therefore, to life."* How have I experienced my body today?

This experience felt

- ☐ painful
- ☐ comfortable
- ☐ distressing
- ☐ difficult
- ☐ easy

*Amodeo, *Dancing with Fire*, 14.

"Happiness, knowledge, not in another place but this place,
not for another hour but this hour."*

—WALT WHITMAN

Do some Sun Salutations. Feel how moving and stretching your muscles feels as you explore the edge around and beyond your comfort zone, finding that sweet spot and stopping just before you feel any pain.

*In Cantoni, "Walt Whitman, Secular Mystic," 379–84.

# 10
## DECEMBER

Have you ever observed children when they are absorbed in a creative activity? Very often they will delight in choosing a crayon and enthusiastically explain what they are drawing. But with time, we might lose courage as we receive negative messages externally, and then internally. As you color in the mandala below, can you connect to your choice of color and how it feels to be in this moment as you experience your creativity unfurl? Could you put your finished drawing somewhere where you will see it? If self-critical thoughts come up, just notice them. Like a loving parent, praise yourself for your work of art.

What mindfulness practice did I do today? What did I notice, and what meaning did it have for me? As the holiday season approaches, take stock of any addictive behaviors or habits on this list:

- ✦ alcohol
- ✦ tobacco, vaping
- ✦ recreational drugs
- ✦ painkillers/sleeping pills
- ✦ internet surfing
- ✦ overworking/overachieving
- ✦ shopping
- ✦ cleaning
- ✦ eating
- ✦ exercising
- ✦ soft drinks
- ✦ performing

What are the fears that fuel these behaviors? What are you avoiding feeling with these smokescreens?

# 12
## DECEMBER

Did you know that women may become less sociable during menopause? This is not necessarily a bad thing and may be a way for women to allow themselves time for introspection and looking after their own needs before others'. Instead of asking yourself today what's wrong, how about putting on your gratitude glasses and asking what's right?

Skin can become drier during menopause. The good news is that acne and blemishes are a thing of the past. Upgrade your cream to a richer texture. Facial oils can be a quick and pleasant way to moisturize a clean face before bed. Take this moment to enjoy the smell and texture of the cream or oil as you massage it in with gentle, caring strokes.

## THE THIEF OF SLEEP

She lies in her bed
like a butterfly
captured in its cocoon,
waiting for dawn
to acquit her.
But when the
light comes
her wings will have
grown still.

So in the sweltering
silence she decides
that she will no longer
squirm.
She surrenders
to the frightening peace,
and even beckons it in.

Instead of fighting
to escape, she peels
back the layers

within, one by one,
experiencing the subtle feelings
and observing what
kindness brings.

Instead of struggling
with her confines,
she listens to her body
with love,
becomes present in the moment.
Simply being her body softens
as she snuggles in
and wraps herself in
tender wings,
like a pearl within a shell.
And her thumping
heart becomes
a melodic tambour.
And her panting breath
a calm blue shore
drifting her to sleep.

Before bed, give yourself a few minutes to do a few slow yoga poses, evacuating any tension that has built up during the day. This small ritual can become your "fun salutations."

"We are like islands in the sea, separate on the surface
but connected in the deep."*

Do a few minutes of yoga from the sequence for energy at the back of the book.
(Some poses for energy might be Eagle or any of the Warrior poses.) If you are
feeling tired, ask yourself where it is coming from. Is it physical, mental, or emotional?

*Roudeau, "Like Islands in the Sea," 190–216.

# 16
## DECEMBER

Did you know that your breath is your brain's remote control? Inhaling a deep breath through the nose (and not through the mouth) allows you to be more emotionally aware and improves memory. Exhaling has a calming effect on the sympathetic nervous system, so it reduces stress and anxiety. Be aware of the length of your inbreath and outbreath.

How am I sleeping?

☐ Well

☐ Average

☐ Poorly

If sleep has become compromised, could you commit to some of the poses in the yoga sequence for sleep at the back of the book, such as Standing Forward Bend, Cobbler's Pose, or Wide-Knee Child's Pose? Which poses did you try? How did you experience the poses and movement?

_____

_____

_____

_____

_____

_____

_____

_____

_____

_____

_____

# 18
## DECEMBER

"Meditation is intended to purify the mind. It cleanses the thought process of what can be called 'psychic irritants,' things like greed, hatred, and jealousy, which keep you snarled up in emotional bondage. Meditation brings the mind to a state of tranquillity and awareness, a state of concentration and insight."*

*Gunaratana, *Mindfulness in Plain English*, 8.

"It is the everlasting and unchanging rule of this world that everything is created by a series of causes and conditions and everything disappears by the same rule; everything changes, nothing remains constant."*

Choose a meditation. How was the experience of this meditation?

*Kyōkai, *The Teachings of Buddha*.

## 20
DECEMBER

Today, listen to your environment as attentively and acutely as possible. Note below your thoughts and behaviors in response to certain sounds.

| SOUND | THOUGHT | BEHAVIOR |
|-------|---------|----------|
|       |         |          |
|       |         |          |
|       |         |          |
|       |         |          |
|       |         |          |
|       |         |          |
|       |         |          |

As Christmas approaches, I would like you to mindfully ponder what this occasion means for you if you do or don't celebrate it. This year, I invite you to celebrate Christmas mindfully rather than having an unthinking commercial orientation to the holiday or making it an exercise in overindulgence. Focus on making it a time to change your routine or tradition slightly, and make it a chance to spend time with those you care about with the greatest present, your presence. What would help you to make this occasion more memorable and less stressful?

# 22
## DECEMBER

*Rebecca found that since going into menopause she was a lot more impatient—for instance, when she couldn't find something in her home that her partner had put away or during calls with her aging mother. One quality she developed through meditation was patience.*

Allow waiting to be an opportunity to stretch your spine as high as you can, then release the breath, keeping your core engaged after finishing the stretch.

Sometimes establishing a ritual or a habitual practice is the easiest way to maintain a regular meditation and yoga practice. How might you be able to make yoga and meditation an essential part of your day?

 Times for the 3-minute
meditation today:

1. _____

2. _____

3. _____

# 24

"Breathing in, I calm the body and mind. Breathing out, I smile.
Dwelling in the present moment, I know this is the only moment."
—THICH NHAT HANH, *The Miracle of Mindfulness*

What might be the benefit today of doing things in a calm manner? What happened today when you did something hastily or rashly?

_____

_____

_____

_____

_____

_____

_____

_____

_____

_____

_____

_____

_____

_____

_____

_____

_____

_____

*Suzanna mentioned in a therapy session before Christmas, "Christmas has always been a source of stress for me. I exhaust myself battling through the supermarket, buying too much, spending more than I can afford. Gift buying is another source of stress. By the time I sit down to eat Christmas lunch, I am exhausted, grouchy, and just want it to be over. With the advent of my menopause, I have even less stamina and patience, and quite frankly I am dreading it!"*

Whether you celebrate Christmas or not, today make an extra effort to turn the day into one of love and connection. Reflect on the following: What really matters for me right now in my life? What experience could make this day memorable? What has been a source of stress for me today? How can I kindly and tactfully change this? How can I communicate this to those whom I will share this moment with?

Some helpful tricks:

1. Try not to overeat. Enjoy a little of everything but keep portions small.
2. If there is heating or a log fire, dress in layers with a cotton t-shirt or shirt underneath.
3. Allow yourself a nap if you are tired.
4. Go for a nice long walk with family members and enjoy nature.
5. Keep a jug of festively decorated (e.g., orange slices and cinnamon sticks) water with ice at hand and hydrate throughout the day.
6. If you drink, keep alcoholic beverages and coffee to a minimum.

Wherever you are in the world, whatever you believe in and celebrate, come home to your present experience, right here, right now.

"Breath is the bridge which connects life to consciousness, which unites your body to your thoughts."

—THICH NHAT HANH, *The Miracle of Mindfulness*

Can you find time for a full yoga sequence? Use self-study (*svadyaya*) during your sequence to observe your breath. What is it telling you? Are you holding your breath when making an effort? What emotions are connected to the postures—sadness, anger, fear, boredom, frustration, or joy, compassion, surrender? Don't push them away, just notice what comes up.

One thing yoga taught me is that if I am feeling overwhelmed, I come back to the beginner's mind. Whether on my meditation cushion, blanket, or yoga mat, I quickly feel cooler, calmer, and collected.

Today I suggest a *pranayama* (breathing) exercise to calm an agitated mind.

1. Sit down in easy pose.
2. The left hand is placed on the left knee in gyan mudra.
3. The right hand goes in front of the nose.
4. The right thumb closes the right nostril.
5. The other fingers point upward.
6. Breathe slowly and deeply from the belly for about 3 minutes.
7. Close both nostrils, gently holding the breath in.
8. Squeeze the root lock (Mula Bandha), with light neck lock (Jalandara Bandha), so that the chin comes down and the sternum up.
9. Concentrate on the third eye.
10. Slowly release your right hand onto your right knee and breathe slowly out of both nostrils. Stay and connect fully with your bodily sensations.

# 28
DECEMBER

Today pay attention to smelling your environment as acutely as possible. What thoughts accompanied certain smells and aromas or perfumes, and what behaviors followed? Smells are tightly connected with emotions and can stir up memories (good and bad) as well as a reaction to go toward or away from. Think of the attraction of a fragrant perfume or the aversion of bad breath or other bodily odors. How can we tame our reactivity through our olfactory senses? How might our aversion to certain smells impact our feelings toward people who smell bad to us, and how might we become more compassionate toward them?

| SMELL | THOUGHT | BEHAVIOR |
|-------|---------|----------|
|       |         |          |
|       |         |          |
|       |         |          |
|       |         |          |
|       |         |          |
|       |         |          |
|       |         |          |

As the end of another year draws near (and as we get older and, we hope, wiser), it's easier to think that the work is done. But live today (and tomorrow and tomorrow's tomorrows) with a beginner's mind. Don't assume you are an expert. Every situation and every time is different.

Do a short meditation with a beginner's mind and connect with your body and breath in silence.

_____

_____

_____

_____

_____

_____

_____

_____

_____

_____

_____

_____

_____

_____

_____

# 30
DECEMBER

If it is winter where you are, a great way to meditate is in front of the fireplace. It's hard not to be in the moment and not enjoy the wonderful sensations of warmth and comfort, the wonderful sounds, and the smell of wood burning. Describe what in your environment allows you to tune in to your meditation.

Congratulations! You've made it through the year! What went well this year? What are you grateful for? What intention could you set for next year?

I hope you enjoyed your journey and look forward to next year with you on another mindfulness exploration.

Bless you and much love,

Francesca

# Meditations

# Meditations

## POSITIONS FOR MEDITATION

A LTHOUGH MEDITATION can be practiced anywhere (and you don't even need to be sitting down), the following positions can help you develop and deepen your practice. Sitting down gives you stability and allows you to focus your attention on the formal object of meditation instead of thinking about balance. It is more restful. By keeping the body still, mental stillness follows.

The important thing is to find the most comfortable position for you personally, the one you can stay in the longest without moving, being in pain, or experiencing any physical trauma. Experiment with different positions and see how your experience changes. With time you will be able to go a little further as your tendons and muscles become more supple.

Sitting on a chair or meditation stool. If mobility is an issue, keep a cushion behind your back so that the back is straight. Don't rest your back against the back of the chair. It is important to be comfortable but relaxed. Feet are flat on the ground, slightly apart.

Sitting on a meditation cushion in easy pose, legs crossed at shins. You may wedge a cushion against the small of your back to rock your pelvis forward and position your knees lower than the hips.

In half-lotus position if that is comfortable.

With knees supported.
Lying down on back (with the forearms up for sleepy meditators).

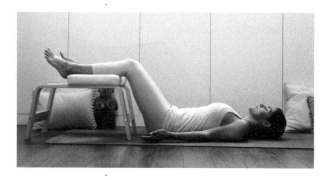

The astronaut position (with forearms up for sleepy meditators, or with forearms down and palms up if you prefer).

Some other meditation suggestions:

Breath: Don't try to control it. Just follow it.

Clothes: Easy, loose styles and soft fabrics work best. Remove shoes and belt and eye glasses.

Eyes: If you want to stay more anchored to your surroundings, you can keep your eyes open, looking straight ahead. If you want to bring your awareness more to your internal sensations, you can close your eyes.

Arms/hands: Let your shoulders relax. Keep your arms hanging down by your trunk. Your hands can rest lightly on your thighs, or you may place your right hand over your left palm, both palms facing upward. If you are lying down, you may keep an arm bent at the elbow in order to avoid falling asleep!

Legs/feet: If you are sitting on a chair, your head should be straight (as if pulled by a string from the ceiling). Your feet should be apart and firmly on the ground.

Back: Your back should be straight (visualize your vertebrae like a stack of coins) and dignified, but not rigid. This is important so that the respiratory airways are free.

Time: The notion of "time" gets distorted when we meditate. You can either listen to a recorded meditation or set a timer to ring at a programmed time. You can increase your sessions gradually. Obviously, quality of focus is important, so you are better off with a short concentrated session than a drowsy 45-minute meditation!

## COMMON OBSTACLES AND CHALLENGES TO MEDITATION

### WANTING TO CHANGE POSITION.

Meditation can be painful, as we are not used to staying still for long periods of time. Stillness needs slow training and patience. Try to experiment with different positions and adjust, but know that meditation should not damage your knees or result in damage. Once you have found a comfortable position, commit to staying there and not fidgeting about. Be present to any residual pain. Explore any resistance or tension in facing the pain. Relax the tension. Now relax mental tension. Mind and body are inextricably linked. If the pain is too much, move slowly and mindfully. Pins and needles is another uncomfortable sensation caused by nerve pinch. It is not dangerous and you don't have to move around. You may experience other strange proprioceptive and interoceptive sensations (both are stimuli produced and perceived within an organism). Don't get wrapped up in them. Just observe them come and go.

### MIND WANDERING.

Your mind will at some point drift into thoughts or toward outside stimuli, distracting you away from the breath and back to the past or the anticipation of future events. As soon as you notice this, calmly guide it back to the breath, as if it were a tethered balloon. If keeping the focus proves difficult, you can mentally count the length of the inbreath, pause, outbreath, and pause. Another way of counteracting the distraction is to roughly estimate the length of time your mind has wandered—for example, I have been thinking about my phone bill for the last 2 minutes—then come back to the breath.

### SLEEP.

This is really quite difficult when you are tired, as meditation can be very calming and relaxing! Find out what might be the cause (a big meal just prior to practicing, strenuous physical activity, poor sleep). Pay attention to the body's needs, then meditate.

## THE RAISIN EXERCISE

For this exercise you will need a raisin. If you dislike raisins, another small dried fruit can be substituted. In fact the exercise can be repeated with any edible object. Find a quiet place where you will not be disturbed. Get into a comfortable position. Put the raisin in the palm of your hand and just observe it generally. Notice its appearance from your outstretched palm.

Now take it between your index finger and thumb and bring it nearer to your eyes. Look at this raisin as if you are an alien who has never seen a raisin before and doesn't even know if it's edible. Notice its color—is it uniform all over? Look at its surface texture—are the wrinkles on its skin similar or different? Turn it over and examine its surface completely. If thoughts come to mind such as "What is the point of this exercise?" just make a mental note of them. Then bring your awareness back to your experience of observing the raisin.

Now bring your awareness to your present experience of touch. Notice the firmness of the raisin or its softness. If you apply a little more pressure on its surface, does it yield and bounce back to shape? Are there any harder parts?

Now bring the raisin near to your nose and notice if the raisin has any particular aroma or smell. If there is none, make a note of this too.

Now very slowly prepare to bring the raisin to your lips, aware of the movement of your hand and arm. Remark how they know exactly how to get to your mouth. You may even close your eyes.

Hold the raisin on your lower lip, feeling the temperature of its surface on your lip. Feel the texture of the raisin's skin on your lip. Now extend the tip of your tongue toward the raisin. Be aware if your mouth salivates slightly in anticipation. Let the raisin move onto the tongue. Don't chew it, just hold it on your tongue and observe if there are any changes. Move it around your mouth and see if there are any different perceptions of taste. Now bring the raisin between your front teeth and bite down on the raisin once. Explore any changes in taste on different parts of the tongue. Now chew the raisin slowly. Feel the change in the raisin's texture. Slowly swallow the pulp with full awareness of the movement of your throat muscles and any sensations in your stomach. If there are none, notice that too.

## ABDOMINAL BREATHING

Find a space where you will not be disturbed for a few minutes. Get into a comfortable position lying either on an exercise mat or on blankets. If this is not comfortable for you, you may rest your feet on a chair and have your knees bent at 90 degrees. You may also sit on a chair with a blanket supporting your back if lying down is not an option for you.

Without wanting to control or change anything, bring your gentle awareness to your abdomen as it rises with each inbreath and falls with each outbreath, naturally and effort-lessly. Just observe your breath from moment to moment, gently bringing your attention back to the breath when the mind wanders.

## THREE-MINUTE BREATHING SPACE

It would be great if this could become a regular practice three times a day, perhaps at reg-ularly recurring moments: upon awakening, during a coffee break, and before getting into bed. Start by adopting an erect and dignified posture, standing or sitting, straight, light, and easy. You may close your eyes. Direct your attention to your inner experience. Ask your-self, "What am I experiencing right now?" "What thoughts are going through my mind?" Acknowledge these thoughts as mental events, perhaps naming them briefly. What feelings are there? Acknowledge their presence and whether they are emotionally uncomfortable or unpleasant.

Bring your attention then to bodily sensations. Quickly scan your body and recognize any physical sensations. Now bring your awareness to the physical sensations of breathing. Sense the breath in the tummy area as the air enters the lungs and the abdominal wall expands. Feel the lungs slowly empty themselves of air and the abdominal wall lowering. Allow your breath to anchor you to the present moment. If your mind wanders. Let the breath bring it back. Now expand the field of your awareness around your breath so that it includes the whole body from head to toe. As best you can, bring this expanded awareness to your day.

## FIVE-MINUTE MINDFUL BREATHING MEDITATION

Find a quiet place. You can sit down if you feel sleepy or lie down if you are more energized. Guide your attention to the sensations of your body—the temperature in different parts, the weight of your body, or the feeling of your clothes. You may feel discomfort and want to rearrange your posture, and you may do so now.

Take three deep breaths. Now breathe normally, breathing in through your nose and out from your mouth, allowing your breath to flow effortlessly in and out of your body. Focus your attention on the entrance to your nostrils. Perhaps you can sense a difference in temperature as the air enters through the nostrils and exits, or exits from the mouth. Feel your ribs and belly expand. Now bring your awareness to the pauses between each inhale and each exhale. Normally you might not be aware of these pauses, but with mindfulness you can be.

Your mind might be drawn to distracting thoughts; it's normal, just bring your attention back to your breath. If you find the task difficult or start judging yourself, just come back to each breath.

It is challenging to think of nothing. The mind is forever being pulled here and there, but just refocus on your breath, allowing it to be natural. Each time you catch your mind wandering is an opportunity to become attuned to your growing awareness. You may notice that as you become still and settled, the length of your breath becomes longer and deeper. If this is not the case, just observe.

## Five-Minute Self-Compassion Break

Bring to mind a difficult situation related to your menopause. It may be at work, at home with your partner, or elsewhere. Reconnect with this difficulty. Say to yourself, "This is a difficult moment for me as a woman. It is tough and I am struggling. Suffering is part of life. It's not abnormal to be going through this. Many women struggle with this. It is common. I am not alone."

Now say to yourself, "May I be kind and gentle to myself." Put your hands on your heart, on your tummy or on your cheeks, or wherever feels reassuring for you, and feel the warmth and care radiating toward you. Say to yourself in a calm and genuine voice, "I am here and I care. I am doing my best." You can use your nickname or a term of endearment that feels natural for you. "May I be well and free from the difficulties that I am going through." Acknowledge the difficulties and allow yourself to be just as you are in this moment.

## Walk the Mindfulness Walk— Ten-Minute Walking Meditation

This meditation can be an informal practice, bringing awareness to this everyday activity whenever getting around on foot. It can also be a formal practice. Walking provides an opportunity to bring ourselves back from mental time travel to the past or future or when we drift into autopilot. To start with, find a place where you will be left alone. It could be in a park, the woods, a forest, or even in a building (long corridor).

Let your arms remain loose and comfortable at your sides or crossed loosely behind your back. With each step, pay attention to the sensation as each foot lifts from the ground (heel of the foot, front of the foot, toes) and when each foot is placed on the ground. Feel the shift of weight from leg to leg. Notice the sounds around you as nothing more than sound. No need for naming, qualifying, or labeling.

Now expand your awareness to what you see in your environment. Neither rigidly focusing on anything nor avoiding anything, just be present to the colors and textures around you.

Now move your awareness to smells. Just let smells come to you.

In the last few minutes, return your awareness to the sensations of your movement and the ground under your feet. When you are ready to bring your walking meditation to an end, stop and stand still for a moment.

## Metta (Loving-Kindness) Meditation

Get into a comfortable position. Take a slow, deep breath in. Now let the breath out until you have completely exhaled. Take another deep breath in. Now let it out slowly. Feel the breath radiating in your chest around your heart area.

Mentally repeat, "May I be peaceful, well, and free from suffering." As you say this, connect with the intention. You may picture yourself as you say this.

Now bring to mind someone who has deeply cared for you. Repeat the phrase, "May you be peaceful, well, and free from suffering."

Now bring to mind acquaintances or a neutral person. Recalling that person, say to yourself, "May you be peaceful, well, and free from suffering."

Now think of someone with whom you have fallen out or had conflict or difficulty. Recalling that person, say to yourself, "May you be peaceful, well, and free from suffering." It will be difficult at the beginning and anger, rage, or disappointment may arise. Don't judge yourself for having these emotions. You can do this meditation wherever you are and if someone is pushing your buttons!

Now think of humanity all over the planet. Say to yourself, "May all people on this planet be peaceful, well, and free from suffering."

Truly participate in these utterances, investing them with all the positive energy that you have at this moment. If it is difficult right now, be patient, be compassionate. It will get easier with practice.

## Body-Scan Meditation

Once you have read this and are familiar with the procedure, you can set a timer on a phone for 20 minutes. This healing and powerful meditation is to help you discover your body as if it were a new territory. The potential side effect is falling asleep, or at least feeling sleepy, so if you are lying down, it can help to keep an arm up to alert you if you do nod off. Doing the body scan when you are well rested in the morning can also help fight falling asleep. As we get in touch with our body, we can use this meditation to fall awake!

Lying down can help us feel supported and encourage us to surrender to gravity. So get into Corpse Pose, lying down on your back with arms by your sides and legs straight and slightly turned outward. To start with, bring your loving attention to the toes of your left foot. Now expand this focus to the sole, the heel, and the front of your left foot. Now direct your attention to the left ankle. Slowly bring the attention upward toward the left shin, then move the attention to the calf, the knee, the front of the thigh, the back of the thigh, the whole thigh. Now draw the attention to the groin, then the left hip, attending to the sensations in this area.

Now focus your attention on the toes of the right foot, the sole, the front of the foot, then the ankle. Now focus on the shin of the right leg, then the knee. Move your attention to the front of the right thigh, then the back of the thigh; the groin of the right leg, then the hip of the right leg. Now bring your attention to the pelvic region and feel any sensations there. Then bring awareness to the genitals, the buttocks, the lower back, the upper back. Feel any tension or clenching. Now draw attention to the tummy area, where we often feel sensations brought on by intuitive awareness or stress. Now bring the attention upward toward the ribs, then the breasts—an area where hormonal changes can be acutely felt by some women. Now focus on the lungs—the rising and expansion with each inbreath and the lowering and decreasing volume with each outbreath. Now notice the heart area. Perhaps you can feel your heart beating. Then the area around your collarbone, and your shoulders, where tension can build up in times of stress. Be aware of the heaviness and looseness of this area. Now bring your attention to the left arm, the forearm, the wrist, the fingers and the palm. Go back up the left arm and across the shoulder blades to the right arm. The right forearm, wrist, fingers, and palm. Go up the right arm to the back of the neck, and to the back of the head and the scalp. Feel any remaining tension there. Now bring your awareness to the face. Release any micro tension around the forehead, the eyes, and the mouth.

Finally bring your attention globally to the whole body, from the head to the toes. Breathe long and deeply for three breaths.

When the chime sounds, you can open your eyes and bring your awareness back to your surroundings.

## GUIDED MEDITATION TO GET TO SLEEP

Perhaps your mind is full of chatter—thoughts that come in, judgments, regrets, things that seem so pressing right now. These thoughts are called "rumination," and everybody experiences them to a lesser or greater extent.

Lie down in your bed on your back, or find a position that is comfortable for you. When you wish, you may let your eyelids relax and close. Bring your awareness to your breath, feeling your lungs, your diaphragm muscles, and your stomach rising and falling with each breath. Feel your ribs expand and contract with each breath. Feel the sensation of the air entering your nostrils, warming as you inhale it, and going into your lungs. Not forcing anything but just allowing your body to do what it does naturally. Bring your attention to the temperature in different parts of your body. There is no wrong or right way to do this, just allow your attention to travel calmly to each part of your body. These sensations may change, and that is completely normal as you allow your body to rest. Become aware of any residual tension or tightness. Don't force anything, just greet this tension and let your breath guide you slowly. There is no rush, nowhere to go. This time is for you, well earned, and it allows you to reacquaint yourself with your body's needs and reactions in this moment.

You are learning how to rest, being present and positively anchored to the here and now. Your breathing continues naturally and calmly. Observe your breath and allow each breath out to grow comfortably longer and slower.

If thoughts keep coming back, just let them be there, like clouds in the sky, without having to analyze them. Just let them drift along. As your body becomes calmer, your breath is gentle and comfortable. Your attention to your breath is reassuring and comfortable, and you can even count the length of each inbreath and each outbreath and perhaps whether the pause in between is continuous or not.

Your mind may want to come back to thoughts, but gently tell yourself that you will allow yourself time in the day to deal with them and now your calm rest is more important.

Let your attention go to the weight of your body on the surface of where you are lying. Feel if some parts are heavier or lighter than others. Feel the temperature of the sheets. Any excess heat can be slowly released through your mouth as you breathe out.

Just allow yourself this time and space to be. Nowhere to go, nothing to do. If thoughts come back, let them float away. No need to control thinking or change thoughts. Let them be there and give them space in your observation. Acknowledge their presence as "thoughts" and let them fade away like clouds in the sky. You are so much more than your thoughts. Your thoughts are not you.

Let your awareness return simply and easily to your breath, and feel the sensations of your tummy rising and falling gently, rhythmically, and naturally. Let your breath do what it does naturally and comfortably and just observe silently, calmly, and patiently.

Allow each breath to dissipate your thoughts, learning better and better how to allow calmness and comfort to grow within as the space within and outside you seems to give you more freedom. Allow your mind that is usually so busy to just take some time off as you remain anchored to the present and release yourself to drift into a comfortable and restful sleep.

# Yoga

# Yoga Poses

Yoga (lit. "union") is a term that has become common in the West for a group of physical, mental, and spiritual practices originating in ancient India. Yoga is for the mind as much as for the body. Hatha yoga, the practice that Westerners are most familiar with, is a school of yoga that works on balancing and uniting opposites.

If you have any health problems, be sure to check with your health provider first for what range of motion and intensity is suitable. I have indicated levels of difficulty of the postures (L1 being the easiest, L2 intermediate, and L3 the most challenging). Each position can be adapted to your particular needs with props (yoga blocks, bolsters, a yoga strap or jelly pads for delicate knees or hands). As you attempt the following postures, remember it is important to remain focused and present during the movement and the transitions from one posture to another. Instead of observing yourself, experience your body. If it feels wrong, listen to your body. Respect it but also try to explore the limits of your comfort zone when it feels OK. Always check in with your spine. Keep it elongated and supported by your engaged abdominal muscles. Let the breath lead the movement. As a rule of thumb, as you rise, lighten, lengthen, and open, and inhale. As you fold, twist, curl, or ground, exhale. Try to keep the inbreath and outbreath equal. If you are getting out of breath, take a Child Pose, then continue. Breathe through your nose, unless otherwise indicated. I have not indicated times to stay in the poses or repetitions because I want to encourage you to equate awareness with strength. Where there is awareness and knowledge of your anatomy and its ranges of movement, coupled with pleasure in experiencing the energy that is there in the moment, returning to your mat will become a daily appealing ritual and benefit your health holistically.

Yoga is best done first thing in the morning if you have the time, but any time is good. Do your practice with an empty stomach. Move through the postures slowly. Going slowly becomes even more important as we get older, especially in the morning when the body is stiff after sleep. Feel free to experiment with different sequences. Be graceful, think of symmetry and the balance between effort and ease. Enjoy!

On the following pages you will find instructions and the variations and levels of each pose. The poses are coded to show benefits for muscles, nerves, and tendons; bodily organs and systems; and mental/psychological health. Feel free to progress at your pace.

## Standing Poses

### Mountain Pose (*Tadasana*) (L1)

It is good to start your daily practice with Mountain Pose (*tada* = mountain, *asana* = pose) as a strong foundation upon which to build. Connect with your breath and gauge how you are feeling.

*Benefits*: Comfortable stretching of the muscles; tones muscles of the abdomen, legs, and spine; improves posture. Calms sympathetic system. Increases concentration, awareness.

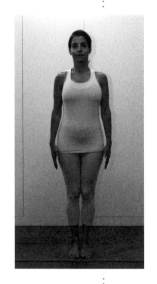

Legs are straight, feet slightly apart. The core lower abdominal muscles are engaged, the navel pulled in. Back is straight. Pelvis is neither tilted backward with caving in of the chest nor is there too much curvature in the lower back. Gaze is focused ahead. You may close your eyes to go within yourself and feel a little more challenged by trying to keep your balance. Shoulders are relaxed. Stand up straight but keep your muscles relaxed. Remain still.

Focus on your inbreath and outbreath, and on your balance, feeling the weight distributed on all parts of the soles of your feet and toes. Play around with this and feel the change in balance elsewhere (too much at the front, back, or one side). Focus on what you can see without looking around or concentrating too hard. Ground yourself in your environment. Imagine a line pulling your head upward and straightening you, as if you were wearing a crown. Try playing with minimal variations until you find a relaxed but dignified posture.

### Variations:

(1) Experiment with tilting the pelvis forward and backward and tightening the pelvic floor. Eyes

can be open or closed, and hands can be held in prayer at the heart center in *Namaste*. Establish an equal, still, steady attention and stance (*sama* = same, *sthiti* = to establish, to stand). Arms can also be hanging down by sides, with palms open toward the front. Stay in the posture for about 1 minute.

(2) If balance is difficult, try it against a wall.

(3) With arms stretched out at shoulder level, parallel to the ground.

### Neck Rolls (*Kantasanchalasana*) (L1–2)

*Benefits*: Strengthens and tones the neck muscles and upper back. Release of tension and stiffness. Great for women who are in front of computer screens all day. Tightens the area under the chin.

With feet slightly apart, back straight, shoulders down, collarbones wide, inhale and bring the chin down gently toward the chest and hold for 1 to 2 seconds, then exhale and raise the head to an upright position. Repeat 1 to 2 times. Do the same movement to the back, the left, the right. Then roll the neck gently to the left, pause; to the front with head tilted down, pause; to the right with head tilted, pause; and to the back, pause. Focus on any tension or pain. Adapt the movement.

VARIATIONS:

(1) You can also do this exercise sitting at a desk at work to relieve tension.

(2) You can make the movement a slow, smooth, continuous circle, exhaling when the head comes down, inhaling when the head comes up. (L2)

### Side Bend in Mountain Pose (*Parshva Tadasana*) (L1)

*Benefits*: Stretches and strengthens side, waist, and oblique muscles; stretches and strengthens lower back and psoas muscles; improves posture; stimulates spinal nerves; stretches and tones abdominal muscles; strengthens hips, legs, and ankles; tones upper arms.

With feet shoulder distance apart, inhale as you bring your arms up to the ceiling. As you exhale, and keeping the core engaged, slowly bend to the side, stretching out the intercostal space (ribs)

on the opposite side to the bend. Hold the posture for 5 to 10 seconds. Inhale and come back to neutral position. Repeat the posture on the other side.

VARIATIONS:
(1) One hand on chair.
(2) Both hands on hips.
(3) Softening alternate knees.
(4) Reach straight up with one hand, as if picking an apple off a tree. Hips must be square and back flat.
    (4a) Twist the wrist as if unscrewing a light bulb.
    (4b) Stretch the opposite leg, pointing the opposite toes like a ballerina and stretching upward.

### SHOULDER SHRUGS (L1)
*Benefits*: Tension release; strengthens the back; relieves shoulder, neck, and trapezoidal pain and headaches.

With the back straight and tall, shoulders down, collarbones wide, inhale to lift the shoulders up toward the ears, squeeze shoulder blades together, hold for a second, exhale and bring the shoulders down and shoulder blades away from each other. Perform 4 to 6 times.

VARIATIONS:
(1) At work sitting down.
(2) Rotating shoulders in a full circle backward, then forward.
(3) Alternate shoulder shrugs.

### TORSO TWISTS IN MOUNTAIN POSE (*PARIVRITTA TADASANA*) (L1)
*Benefits*: Warms up the spine; releases heat and tension; strengthens and tones the shoulders, arms, upper back, and chest.

Standing in Mountain Pose, feet shoulder distance apart, with hands on the hips, breathe in and slowly rotate the chest, shoulders, and head toward the right and backward as if looking behind you. Navel and hips stay facing forward. Take 5 breaths in and out, slowly bringing the head, shoulders, and chest to the front on an exhale. Repeat on the other side.

VARIATIONS:

(1) At work sitting down.

(2) Arms out with elbows away from body, slightly bend the knees as you twist and coordinate your breath with the movement.

(3) Arms out as if holding a hula hoop, twist hips, lift ankle, and point toes, transferring slight weight to different parts of the toes as you move the trunk and arms backward as if looking behind you.

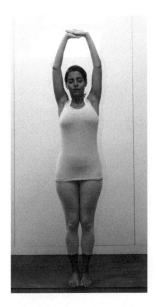

### PALM TREE POSE (*TALASANA*) (L1)

*Benefits*: Keeps your spine long and flexible (great for counteracting the gravitational pull of spine shortening that can lead to slipped discs). Strengthens the oblique muscles—goodbye love handles and muffin tops! Improves balance. Relieves constipation.

Stand straight. Inhale and raise your arms above your head, one hand on top of the other with palms facing the ceiling. Keep your focus in front and steady. Chest is open.

VARIATIONS:

(1) You can also balance on your tiptoes, keeping your balance and stability while holding your breath.

(2) While on your tiptoes, you can also try stepping forward and backward gracefully and slowly.

(3) Swaying Palm Tree (*Tiryaka Talasana*) Open the feet wider than shoulders and, with arms stretched up, sway to left while exhaling, hold the exhale, then straighten to center as you inhale. Now bend to the right while exhaling, hold the exhale, then straighten to center while inhaling. Keep hips square. The movement comes from the waist. If in doubt, perform the movement against a wall.

### UPWARD SALUTE (*URDHVA HASTASANA*) (L1)

Stand in Mountain Pose. Feet are parallel and grounded. Inhale, straightening your body and raising your arms high above your head while arching your back and neck as if reaching for something above and slightly behind. Stretch and expand the rib cage from all sides. Hold the core. Lengthen the tailbone down. Breathe gently and softly. If you are comfortable you can place your gaze on the hands.

VARIATIONS:

(1) Sitting on a chair with back firmly supported.
(2) With a progressive amount of bend backward and arms in different positions. (L3)

### FIVE-POINTED STAR (*UTTHITA TADASANA*) L1

*Benefits*: Tones the arms, waist, and abdominal region and hips; opens the chest.

Standing with feet together, on an exhale step wider apart than shoulders, pointing toes diagonally to the two corners of the mat, then inhale, lifting arms straight out at sides parallel to the ground. Hold the pose a few seconds. Eyes may close. Breathe in. Exhale while lowering the arms to the side of the body and step your feet together.

VARIATIONS:

(1) Start by doing the posture with your back against the wall. This will help keep your back straight and improve balance.
(2) Palms facing up, rotate shoulders, so that palms face downward.

### EXTENDED TRIANGLE POSE (*UTTHITA TRIKONASANA*) (L2)

*Benefits*: Stretches and strengthens neck, spine, shoulders, arms, thorax, hips, groin, knees, hamstrings, ankles. Good for reducing love handles. Improves digestion and reduces pain. Relieves stress.

⚠️ For those with high blood pressure, keep gaze down.

Beginning in a standing position, step your feet three feet apart. Feet are parallel. Raise your arms to shoulder height, palms down. Tighten the right gluteus muscle. Do not lock knees. As you exhale, slowly bend from the waist to the right as the right hand reaches the shin of the right leg and your left arm moves upward. Turn the head gently to look upward at your fingers up ahead, or turn your head downward to look toward the hand on your shin. Stay in the position for 5 seconds, increasing to 10, taking deep steady breaths. Inhale as you rise, then exhale and step feet together. Switch sides.

### TREE POSE (*VRIKSHASANA*) (L2)

As we age, good balance and a strong core go a long way.

*Benefits*: Stretches the torso, shoulders, thighs, groin; tones the abdominal muscles; strengthens spine, ankles, and calves; helps sciatica; opens heart area; improves posture. Reduces stress and anxiety; increases concentration.

Standing in Mountain Pose, take a few breaths. Focus your gaze in front of you on something stable. Keep hips even, shoulders down, and hips squared. Feel rooted into the three corners of your foot (heel, big toe, and pinky toe). Begin to shift the weight from the left foot to the right foot. The left foot lifts off the floor. Bend your left knee and with the left hand bring the sole of the left foot onto the inner right thigh, not on the knee. Press with the thigh into the foot and the foot into the thigh, opening the knee to the side. On the inbreath, the arms stretch out above the head with palms meeting. Keep the spine lengthened, the shoulders down, and both hips squared. Take 5–10 slow, deep breaths. On an exhale, bring the left foot slowly to the floor and lower the arms. Repeat on the other side.

VARIATIONS:

(1) Place the foot on the left calf area, or on the ankle if balance is difficult. (L1)

(2) Hands in prayer (*Namaste*), thumbs resting on the sternum.

(3) Against a wall if balance is difficult to begin with.

### EAGLE POSE (*GARUDASANA*) (L2)

*Benefits*: Stretches shoulders, upper back, thighs, and hips; strengthens core, legs, knees, and ankles. Improves digestion; increases circulation to the sex organs. Improves concentration and balance.

Stand in Mountain Pose with feet shoulder distance apart. Focus your gaze at a point in front of you. Put the weight onto your left foot, bending the knees. Lift the right foot while balancing on your left foot. Wrap the right thigh around the left thigh. Pointing your toes downward, hook the toes of your foot behind the shin of the left leg. Keep your balance on the left foot.

Breathe in and stretch your arms in front of you parallel to the ground. Cross your arms in front of your chest with the right arm over the left and bend the arms. The right elbow should be nested in the left elbow so that the upper arms are parallel to the ground. Palms meet and fingers stretch to the ceiling. Squeeze your arms and thighs together, but open the chest. Hold the posture for 15 seconds to a minute, breathing deeply. On an exhale, gently unwrap your leg and the arm and come into Mountain Pose. Breathe. Repeat the posture on the other side.

VARIATIONS:

(1) Hands in prayer (*Namaste*) in front of the sternum. (L1)

(2) Use a wall behind you for support. (L1)

(3) When you become at ease with this posture, experiment with lowering the hips on an inhale. (L2–3)

### EQUESTRIAN/LOW-LUNGE POSE (*ASHVA SANCHALANASANA*) (L2)

*Benefits*: Opens up the chest, heart, and lungs; stretches the back, arms, shoulders, hamstrings, groin, hips, and quadriceps; stretches the knee tendons and ligaments. Improves balance. Reduces body soreness; relieves sciatica. Stimulates digestion.

From Downward Dog inhale deeply. Exhale while taking a large step with the left foot forward, so that your foot lands between your hands. Hips remain aligned facing forward,

with the knee aligned with the ankle. Hold the position for 5 to 6 seconds while breathing. On an exhale, bring the right foot forward to meet the left foot. Inhale and slowly come back up to Mountain Pose. Take a few breaths and repeat on the other side.

VARIATIONS:

(1) One knee on the floor. (L1)

(2) Blocks under hand(s). (L1)

(3) Arms in *Namaste* or locked behind back (L2), or pointing forward and upward to make a line with the body, or backward and down to make a line with the back leg.

(4) Hands on the hips. (L1–2)

(5) With the knee bent at a right angle, the opposite knee comes down on the floor and slides backward. On an inhale, the arms go straight up, cradling the ears and slightly behind. Open chest. Gaze is forward and slightly raised. Exhale and come back to Downward Dog. (L2)

(6) For a deep stretch, one foot on a chair. (L3)

### WARRIOR POSE I (*VIRABHADRASANA I*) (L1–2)

*Benefits*: Stretches the chest, lungs, shoulders, neck, belly, and groin; strengthens and tones the muscles of the back, shoulders, arms, thighs, calves, and ankles; creates space in the spine—good for sciatica. Improves balance and stamina. Improves digestion. Good for insomnia and self-confidence.

Standing in Mountain Pose, on an exhale step about three feet back with the left foot.

With the heels on the same line, turn the left foot 45 degrees to the left. On an inhale raise the arms straight ahead, palms facing each other and the shoulders down. On an exhale, bend the right knee, bringing the knee over the ankle and the thigh parallel to the floor. Keep the gaze steady and the hips square. Take 5 breaths and, on an inhale, put your weight onto the back heel, straighten out the right knee, exhale, and bring both feet together. Bring the arms down. Switch sides.

VARIATIONS:

(1) With hands on the back of a chair for support. (L1)

(2) With the back foot against a wall for support. (L1)

(3) Try different hand variations—that is, cactus arms (L1), airplane arms (L1), or holding a strap behind the thighs with both hands (L2).

(4) Make the stride larger to add intensity. (L2)

### WARRIOR POSE II (*VIRABHADRASANA II*) (L1)

What better way to feel empowered than becoming a peaceful warrior!

*Benefits*: Stretches the arms, chest, legs, groin. Strengthens the legs and arms, decreases muscle tension. Improves balance; increases groundedness. Improves circulation and digestion; energizes the whole body. Increases physical and emotional strength and develops concentration.

Facing the long side of your mat, in Mountain Pose, on an exhale take a large step to the side with the right foot while raising the arms straight in line with the long edge of the mat, parallel to the ground at shoulder height. Simultaneously, pivot the right foot 90 degrees and the left foot 45 degrees. The right foot and knee should be facing the front of the mat. On an exhale, bend the right knee, keeping the left leg straight. The bent knee should be above the ankle, perpendicular to the floor. The hips should be facing the long side of the mat, as should the straight leg. Keep the gaze forward, looking out at the pointed hand. Stay in the posture for six deep, slow breaths. Inhale, straightening the bent knee. Exhaling, step the feet together. Release the arms down. Come back to Mountain Pose. Repeat on the other side.

VARIATIONS:

(1) Easier: with hands in prayer mudra.

(2) Turn palms up and down, parallel to the mat.

## WARRIOR POSE III (*VIRABHADRASANA III*) (L3)

*Benefits*: Strengthens the whole back side of the body (including the shoulders, back, glutes, hamstrings, quadriceps, calves, and ankles); tones the abdominal muscles; aligns the spine. Stimulates the organs; improves digestion. Improves posture, balance, coordination. Improves concentration.

Standing in Mountain Pose, exhale and bring the right foot 12 inches forward. Put your weight onto the left leg. Inhale and bring the arms straight above the head. On an exhale, slowly raise the right leg straight behind while pivoting at the hips and bringing the arms and chest forward. The core is engaged.

Keep your gaze on a fixed point on the floor to keep your balance. The trunk, stretched out leg, and arms should be parallel to the ground. The supporting left leg should be perpendicular. I like to imagine the letter T. Hold the position for 30 seconds to 1 minute, taking deep, slow breaths. Inhale as you rise, exhale as your lower your arms and right leg down. Take a few breaths then switch sides.

VARIATIONS:

(1) Arms extended out to the side like an airplane. (L2)
(2) Easier: hands resting on a table/chair back at same height as the horizontal spine. (L1)

## STANDING FORWARD BEND (*UTTANASANA*) (L2)

*Benefits*: Stretches the hips, hamstrings, calves; strengthens the thighs and knees; keeps your spine strong and flexible. Relieves tension in the spine, neck, and back. Activates the

abdominal muscles; enhances digestion and decreases constipation. Reduces stress, anxiety, depression, and fatigue; calms the mind and relaxes the nerves; allows fresh blood to the brain, so helps brain fog. Reduces insomnia. Good for high blood pressure and osteoporosis.

Standing with parallel feet, exhale as you lift the arms upward. Exhale, bend forward from the hips with a straight back and engaged core. Drop the upper body as close to the legs as comfortably possible. The hands should make a semi-circle till they touch the floor with the palms. Lift the sitting bones toward the ceiling. Keep the position for 30 seconds to 1 minute, breathing deeply. Inhaling, slowly come up.

VARIATIONS:

(1) Try to rest your torso on the front of your thighs with your head in between the shins. Hold on to the calves or ankles. On each outbreath, try to point the small of the back toward the ceiling and the head toward the floor. (L3)

(2) Knees bent if your hamstrings are too tight or if you experience any tension or pain in the back. (L1)

(3) Hands on blocks close to the feet for those who lack flexibility, so that fingertips do not need to touch floor. (L1)

(4) Using the back of a chair or wall to come down halfway. (L1)

### REVOLVED WIDE-LEGGED FORWARD FOLD (*PARIVRITTA PRASARITA PADOTTANASANA*) (L1)

*Benefits*: Stretches lower back and spine, hips, hamstrings, and calves; strengthens upper back and shoulders; tones abdominal organs.

Stand with feet together. Step your feet at least shoulder distance apart. On an inhale bring arms to shoulder height. On an exhale, bring the head and torso down as the right hand reaches to the left foot. The left arm points to the ceiling. Turn your head left to gaze at the hand pointing upward. Breathe deeply and slowly while holding the pose. Inhale and rise slowly. Exhale and lower the arms, and step the feet together. Repeat on the other side.

VARIATIONS:

(1) Both hands toward one foot. (L2)

(2) Right hand on right ankle, left hand on left ankle. (L2)

## SITTING POSES

### STAFF POSE (*DANDASANA*) (L1)

*Benefits*: Improves posture; strengthens the back muscles and abdominal muscles, shoulders and chest; lengthens and stretches the spine and hamstrings; increases strength and stamina. Stimulates the ovaries and uterus. Relieves menopausal symptoms. Calms stress and mild depression, develops focus and patience.

Sitting with legs together stretched in front on the floor, press hands into the mat, fingers pointed forward. The back is straight. Reach up through the crown of the head, shoulder blades draw together, spine is long, pelvis tilts forward, thighs press down. Press down heels, feet flexed, toes spread pointing to the ceiling. You can increase the challenge by taking 10 breaths while tightening the pelvic floor muscle as you exhale and releasing as you inhale. Release the pose with an exhale.

VARIATIONS:

(1) Sitting on a blanket to support the lower back.

(2) Against a wall.

(3) With blocks under the hands.

### REVOLVED HEAD-TO-KNEE POSE (*PARIVRITTA JANU SHIRSHASANA*) (L2)

*Benefits*: Stretches back, shoulders, torso, and hamstrings. Affects kidneys and liver; stimulates the ovaries and uterus. Relieves menstrual discomfort and menopausal symptoms. Calms stress and mild depression.

Sit comfortably. Stretch your right leg to the side and bring your left heel into your pelvic region. Exhaling, bend from the torso, stretch your right hand to the right foot, bringing your right elbow to your knee. On an inhale, reach your left arm toward the ceiling over your head. Exhale and lower it. Hold on to the ankle or big toe with your right hand. Keep the chest open and the spine extended. Breathe 5–10 times. On an exhale, slowly release to come back up to a neutral straight spine. Swap sides.

VARIATIONS:

(1) Holding on to the foot of the extended leg, the top hand draws an imaginary arc above the body to hold on to the foot. (L3)
(2) With a strap around the sole of the outstretched foot held in the hand on the same side. (L2)

### COW-FACE POSE (*GOMUKHASANA*) (L2)

*Benefits*: Releases shoulder tension, stretches shoulders, chest, and triceps. Tones the abdominal muscles. Improves circulation in the arms and legs, expands breathing, and is beneficial for the heart.

Sit in Staff Pose with legs stretched in front of you. Bend your knees. Bring your left heel by the side of the right buttock. Place your right knee above the left knee, pushing with your right arm against the right thigh. The sitting bones are grounded on the floor. On an inhale, raise your left arm up against your head. On an exhale, bend the left arm at the elbow, while the right arm bends behind the back, pushing the right elbow in (the closer it comes next to the body, the easier it is). If possible, reach your left hand downward to clasp the fingers of the right hand, reaching upward behind your back. The head should not bend forward. Hold the pose and take a few slow, deep breaths, expanding the chest. Exhale, releasing your arms. Switch sides.

VARIATIONS:

(1) Use a belt or yoga strap to help your hands meet comfortably. (L1)
(2) Shoelace: each hand holds the shin bone of opposite leg (right shin in left hand, left shin in right hand). (L2)
(3) Sitting on a yoga block. (L2)
(4) One leg and one arm folded. (L1)

(5) On an exhale, bring the head, chest, and navel area toward the ground as if there were a plank on your back. The hands can hold feet on each side or reach forward. Lengthen the spine, don't curve it. The movement comes from hips. (L3)

(6) For a more relaxing version, you can lie on your back and cross the right knee over left knee. Bend the legs. With right hand, hold on to the left ankle, and with the left hand hold on to the right ankle. The tighter you pull, the more intense is the stretch to the thighs. (L1–2)

## HALF SPINAL TWIST (*ARDHA MATSYENDRASANA*) (L2)

*Benefits*: Stretches spine and lower back, hips, shoulders, arms, and chest. Improves kidney function, liver, adrenal glands. Refreshes the body. Reduces stress, tension, anxiety, and fatigue.

Sitting with your legs stretched out in front of you, bend your left leg and hook the left foot by your right outer thigh. Bend your right leg and put your right foot by your left buttock. Place the fingertips of your left hand to the floor, as far behind your left side for a comfortable stretch, twisting your torso toward the left. Rest your right forearm on the outer left knee. Gaze slightly behind you to the left. Hold the posture, taking deep, slow breaths. Exhale and unfold to neutral. Breathe and then switch sides.

VARIATIONS:

(1) In the seated position, the forearm can point to the ceiling, elbow locking in bent knee. (L1)

## COBBLER'S POSE/BOUND-ANGLE POSE (*BADDHA KONASANA*) (L1)

*Benefits:* Stretches the inner thighs, knees, and groin. Tones the hamstrings and the calves. Strengthens the spine. Increases the blood supply to the pelvis, lower abdomen, kidneys, and bladder; stimulates the bladder and kidneys; stimulates the abdominal organs, such as the ovaries; good for sexual function. Helps relieve menopausal symptoms and reduces hot flashes. Stimulates the heart and improves general circulation. Reduces stress and mild depression; alleviates fatigue.

Sit on the floor with both legs stretched forward. Let the knees lower to the sides naturally. Draw the heels as close to the groin as is comfortable, soles of the feet together. Bend the knees while drawing the heels as close to the groin as is comfortable, bringing the soles of the feet together and holding them with your hands. Sit up tall. Inhaling, lift and open the chest and draw the shoulders back.

VARIATIONS:
(1) You can give small rhythmic impulses to the knees as if you were a butterfly. (L1)
(2) Blocks under knees. (L1)
(3) Leaning from the hips (not back), bend forward. Chest broad. Pelvis tilts forward and spine lengthens. You can use the elbows to push down gently on the thighs. (L2)
(4) With arms behind. Arms move backward and hands are placed on the mat behind the buttocks. You can use them to gently push your chest out. Gaze forward and take deep, slow breaths. Release on an exhale. (L1)
(4) Supported Reclined Cobbler's pose (*Supta Baddha Konasana*): Slowly and mindfully move backward from the initial position with hands behind you to rest on the elbows or a bolster. (L3)

### HEAD TO KNEE POSE (*JANU SHIRSHASANA*) (L1–2)
*Benefits*: Improves the alignment of the spine. Improved digestion, respiration; good for diabetic patients; strengthens weak liver and kidneys; soothes headaches. Calms the nervous system. Reduces fatigue and anxiety.

Sitting down with legs stretched out in front of you, bend the left knee and put the sole of the left foot on the right inner thigh. Flex the right foot. Inhale and raise the arms above the head. Keeping the chest open and the spine elongated and flat, bend from the hips, drawing the belly in while exhaling.

Reach up and forward, with the shoulders open. Hold and breathe deeply and slowly. Release and come back up to sitting position on an inhale. Switch legs.

VARIATIONS:

(1) Use a strap or belt around your foot. (L1)

(2) Add intensity by grabbing the sole of the foot or the big toe with the opposite hand while the same-side hand (facing outward) wraps around the hips. (L2)

(3) If it is painful, bend forward toward a chair and rest the upper body on the edge of the chair. (L1)

(4) Put a rolled-up towel or bolster under the knee. (L1)

(5) Grasp the right ankle with both hands, pressing face to leg. (L3)

### LION POSE (*SIMHASANA*) (L2)

*Benefits*: Lengthens the spine; relieves tension in the face and chest. Prevents sore throat, asthma, and pulmonary problems, improves facial circulation. May help treat bad breath. Relieves anger and irritability.

Kneel on the floor with the knees wide apart. Bring the big toes together. Bring the hips backward toward the heels, but put the weight of the body between the hands. Elbows are straight. Turn the fingers inward and separate the hands shoulder distance apart. Extend the spine and lift the head.

If you wish you can close your eyes and focus your gaze (*drishti*) on the third eye (*Ajna* chakra). If you wish to make the asana even more dramatic, you can stick your tongue out and roar the tension away.

An easier variation is to sit on a chair with legs apart, and open the arms, with the back of the hands touching the knees, palms facing forward and fingers splayed. You can also bring the gaze to the tip of the nose.

## PRONE POSES

### DOWNWARD-FACING DOG (*ADHO MUKHA SHVANASANA*) (L2)

*Benefits*: Stretches the shoulders, back, arms, and legs; strengthens the wrists, arms, shoulders, abdominal muscles, and legs. Helps prevent osteoporosis. Helps maintain the uterus. Increases blood flow to the brain. Improves digestion. Energizing.

Begin on your hands and knees. Arms are straight and shoulder-width apart. Fingers are spread out, palms flat on the floor. Exhale as you tuck your toes under and lift your knees off the floor, straightening the legs. Toes should be pointing forward. Push the floor away from you with your hands. Keep the abs engaged. Try to keep the spine straight and the shoulders down and back. If hamstrings or calves are tight, heels may not touch the floor, though you can pedal your heels up and down alternatively. Lift your bottom toward the ceiling, and gaze toward your shins. Try to visualize a clean inverted V shape. Hold for a minute and try to have 5 deep and equal inbreaths and outbreaths. On an exhale, bend your legs and lower your knees to the floor. Sit back on your heels.

VARIATION:

(1) Holding on to the edge of a chair with a smaller angle of inclination at the hips. (L1)

(2) Bend the knees if the back is weak or the hamstrings are tight. (L1)

(3) A more challenging pose (Three-Legged Downward Dog, or *Tri Pada Adho Mukha Shvanasana*): raise one leg straight and up behind to make a continuous line with the arms, the back, and the lifted leg, then lower. (L3)

**PLANK POSE (*PHALAKASANA*) (L2)**
*Benefits*: Strengthens shoulders, arms, wrists, back, abdominal muscles, and legs, improves balance and posture. Tones abdominal organs. Speeds up metabolism.

⚠ Contraindications: wrist, arms, or shoulder problems.

Start on all fours or from Downward Dog, knees shoulder distance apart and shoulders over wrists, fingers widely apart with palms firmly connected to the ground and middle finger pointing forward. Firm your upper arms in toward each other. Neck is long. Gaze is

downward. Draw the belly up and in. Extend one leg behind and tuck the toes in. Extend the other leg and tuck the toes in. Lift your body up with an engaged abdomen. Don't let the hips dip or rise or bring the head too far up. Imagine a plank on your back. Hold the posture for 10 to 15 seconds. Breathe. Exhaling, relax by lowering the knees, bending the elbows, and bringing the chest to the floor, or going into Downward Dog.

VARIATIONS:
(1) With knees on the floor. (L1)
(2) With feet against a wall. (L2)
(3) With hands slightly open facing away from each other. (L2)
(4) On the forearms if the wrists are sensitive. (L2)

### CAT-COW POSE (*BIDILASANA-MARJARYASANA*) (L1)
*Benefits*: Stretches spine, shoulders, neck, hips. Helps reduce back pain. Improves posture, balance, and coordination. Massages the internal organs. A great exercise for sexual function. Reduces stress, calms the mind, and aids emotional balance.

Start on all fours, with hands firmly on the floor under the shoulders and knees under the hips. Come into a neutral tabletop position. Connect with the natural rhythm of the breath. Draw the navel to the spine on the exhale. The spinal flexion (like an angry cat) produces an exhale as the head slowly moves downward, as if looking in-between legs. Inhale, scoop the heart forward, pushing your belly button toward the ground; the spine is moved downward as the head slowly moves forward and up and the tailbone inclines toward the ceiling.

Think of the movement radiating from the bottom of the spine on the inhale as the head moves up and forward and then from the top of the head down the spine on the exhale, vertebra by vertebra.

VARIATION:
(1) With a yoga block in between the thighs. (L2)

### SUNBIRD POSE (*DANDAYAMANA BHARMANASANA*) (L2)

*Benefits*: Strengthens the arms, wrists, and shoulders; the core muscles, back, and glutes. Improves posture. Stabilizes the pelvis; improves static balance. Increases focus and concentration.

Start on all fours with wrists directly under your shoulders and your knees under your hips. Spread the fingers wide and root down the thumb, index, and pinkie fingers. Bring the gaze slightly in front of the fingers so that the head is in line with the spine. On an inhale, extend the right leg behind, parallel to the floor. With the right arm perpendicular to the floor, inhaling, extend left arm forward, parallel to the floor, palm facing inward in a handshake fashion. Feel a long line of energy from your outstretched hand to your pointed toes. Engage your core. Stay for 30 seconds to a minute. Exhale and bring the arm and leg down. Repeat on the other side.

 Women with knee, shoulder, or wrist injuries should avoid this pose.

VARIATIONS:
(1) Put a blanket under the balancing knee for extra cushioning.
(2) Bend the outstretched leg inward, bending at the knee, so that as it moves forward it meets the elbow of the opposite arm as it moves backward. (L3)

## BACKBENDS

### COBRA POSE (*BHUJANGASANA*) (L2)

*Benefits*: Spinal flexibility. Stimulates the abdominal organs. Relieves stress.

Lie face down on the floor with parallel feet and pointed toes, heals pointing to the ceiling. Press the top of the feet into the mat. Place the hands slightly outside shoulders with spread fingers. Engage legs and stomach. Ground the hips. As you inhale, push your chest forward and up with your hands as your arms straighten. Tilt the head up.

Lengthen the spine, raise the navel off the ground, but the hips remain on the floor. Breathe and hold the pose. Exhale, bend the elbows and lower the navel, shoulders, and forehead to the mat.

VARIATION:

(1) If there are any back issues, reduce the angle of the backbend by resting on the forearms.

## UPWARD-FACING DOG POSE (*URDHVA MUKHA SHVANASANA*) (L2)

*Benefits*: Stretches the spine, chest, and abdomen; strengthens the shoulders, arms, and wrists; improves posture. Stimulates the digestive organs. Fights feelings of being overwhelmed, as it encourages extroversion.

Lie on your stomach. Place your hands on the mat on each side of your torso, under your shoulders. Keep the elbows close to your body. Stretch out your legs at shoulder width, the toes grounded on the mat. Inhale, then push down onto the mat with your hands and the front of the feet. Contract the glutes, pushing the pelvis forward and upward on the mat. Raise the upper body, arms straight. Push the shoulders down and back, chest forward, and straighten out your neck to look in front and upward.

## KING COBRA POSE (*RAJA BHUJANGASANA*) (L3)

*Benefits*: Deep backbend stretches and strengthens the spine, middle back, and upper back; strong stretch of front body (quadriceps, chest, shoulders, and throat); tones and firms the gluteus muscles. Improves digestion, oxygenates the blood, improves circulation, and improves lung function. Elevates mood.

 Avoid if you have back, neck, or wrist injuries.

Lie on your stomach. Place your hands on the mat on each side of your torso, under your shoulders. Keep the elbows close to your body. Spread the legs so the knees reach toward

the edges of the mat. Inhale, then push down onto the mat with your hands and the front of the feet. Contract the glutes, pushing the pelvis forward and upward on the mat. Raise the upper body, arms straight. Push the shoulders down and back, chest forward, and straighten out your neck to look in front and upward. Bend the knees and take the toes toward your head and the center of the mat. Stay for a few breaths, and on the exhale, lower slowly onto the mat.

VARIATIONS:

(1) With a bolster under the lower belly. (L1)

(2) Sitting on the edge of a chair, bring the hands to the edge where the back joins the seat and hold on if it is comfortable. Exhale as you draw the stomach in and raise the chest and gaze up to the ceiling. Exhale, relax. (L1)

### HALF-LOCUST POSE (*ARDHA SHALA-BHASANA*) (L1)

*Benefits*: Strengthens the neck and spine, alleviates slipped discs. Helpful for constipation.

Lie on your stomach. Rest your chin on the floor. The arms are held close to the sides of your body, palms up. On an inhale, firm the left glutes, lift your right leg as high as possible while keeping it straight. The opposite leg stays on the ground. Hold as long as possible, then exhale, lowering the leg. Breathe and then switch legs. Then rest in a prone position in Reverse Corpse Pose, with the head turned to the side. Relax for a few breaths.

VARIATIONS:

(1) Palms under the thighs at the groin. (L1)

(2) Raise both legs off the ground. (L2)

### LOCUST POSE (*SHALABHASANA*) (L1)

*Benefits*: Strengthens the muscles of the spine, buttocks, and backs of the arms and legs. Stretches the shoulders, chest, belly, and thighs. Improves posture. Stimulates abdominal organs. Helps relieve stress and depression.

Lie down on your stomach, arms along your body, palms facing upward. Knees should be facing downward. Forehead on the mat. Tightening the buttocks, inhale and raise the head, chest, and legs off the floor. Open up the chest. Hold the posture for 30 seconds to a minute as you breathe. Exhale and repeat once or twice more.

VARIATIONS:

(1) Raise both legs off the ground, keeping them together. The body should be supported on the pelvis and abdomen.
(2) Clasp the hands behind the back for a deeper stretch of the shoulders and chest.
(3) Arms lengthening forward and up.

### BRIDGE POSE (*SETU BANDHA SARVANGASANA*) (L1)

*Benefits*: Strengthens spine, neck, chest, pelvic area, glutes, and hamstrings; stretches hip flexors, spine. Improves lung capacity; stimulates organs, thyroid; boosts blood circulation; eases back pain; soothes headaches; regulates blood pressure. Energizing, rejuvenating, restorative; pelvic-floor toning; therapeutic for insomnia, osteoporosis, stress, constipation. Reduces stress, anxiety, depression. Eases menopausal symptoms.

Lie on your back. Feet hip distance apart. Bend the knees but don't bring the feet too close to the buttocks. The knees are over the toes and aligned. Arms are extended over the head, pressing into the ground palms up. On an inhale tighten the buttocks as you lift the pelvis, raising the lower and middle back off the floor. Roll out the shoulders. Hold the pose as you breathe in and out deeply. On an outbreath slowly lower the hips.

VARIATIONS:

(1) Arms toward feet, hands clasped under glutes. (L2)

(2) Arms on the floor, holding a strap or belt between hands under the glutes. Gradually move hands closer once the hips have lifted up. (L1)

(3) With a foam block or firm cushion between inner thighs, squeeze lightly. (L1)

(4) With a thin rolled-up towel under your neck to support the curve. (L1)

(5) With arms toward feet, bend arms and support the raised hips by placing one hand under each hip. (L1)

(6) Raising the straight arms up and backward (as if drawing a semi-circle) as the pelvis goes up on the inhale, bringing arms back down on the exhale as the pelvis comes down. (L2)

(8) With a block supporting the back under the sacrum. (L1)

(9) Squeeze the pelvic floor and hold for 30 seconds to 1 minute. (L1)

(10) Engage the core, and on an inhale lift the buttocks off the floor while pointing the right toes to the ceiling. Body weight is distributed on the upper back, shoulders, arms, left foot, and the back of the head. The movement can be done slowly and held (then switch sides) or dynamically and repetitively with a slow pulsing motion for toning. Do a few repetitions and switch sides.

### FISH POSE (*MATSYASANA*) (L2)

*Benefits*: Deep stretch for the shoulders, chest, and front body, including the throat, abdomen, and hip flexors; strengthens the musculature of the back and neck; relieves spinal, shoulder, or neck tension; better breathing; improves posture. Improves the function of the thyroid, parathyroid, pituitary, and pineal glands. Increases vitality and relieves stress.

⚠ Caution is advised for those who have neck or lower back pain.

Lie on your back with legs straight and feet pointed forward. Support the body with forearms, elbows pushed into the floor. Inhale and lift the upper back. Place the crown of the head close to the ground, exhale. There should be a space between the upper back and the ground. The weight is on the elbows, hips, and core. Drop the shoulders,

allowing them to squeeze down. Stay in the pose for 30–60 seconds, breathing deeply and slowly. Exhale, bring the head up, lower the chest and head to the mat, and bring the arms along the sides of the body. Sitting up, you can do a few movements of the head downward toward the chest to counteract the position.

VARIATIONS:

(1) A more challenging version is with legs in lotus position. (L3)

(2) Put a blanket under the head to give extra cushioning. (L1)

(3) Palms closer to the shoulders. (L1)

### CAMEL POSE (*USHTRASANA*) (L3)

*Benefits*: Stretches the abdominal muscles, hips, and thighs; improves flexibility in the thoracic spine; opens the shoulders and chest. Stimulates the thyroid gland (balancing metabolism). Good for sexual function.

Begin on the knees, with knees hip-distance apart. Keep your feet on the ground, rotate your knees inward and shins on the ground. Place your hands on your hips, fingers facing down. Inhaling, lengthen the spine and open your chest. On an exhale, slowly lean back, tucking in your chin comfortably toward your chest. Broaden the shoulder blades; arms should be parallel to each other; upper body lifts from the back ribs. With a deep inhale, slowly reach back and hold on to each ankle. Make sure that your thighs are perpendicular to the floor. Keep your spine long, your chest open, and allow your head to drop back or stay in a neutral position. Hold the pose and take deep, slow breaths. Return

the hands to the back and slowly inhaling, rise, bringing the neck and shoulders back into a neutral position. Sit back on your heels. Child Pose can be a great way to neutralize the pose.

 Be alert to possible dizziness.

VARIATIONS:

(1) Toes curled under so heels are higher. (L2)

(2) Keep hands on buttocks and don't drop your head too far back. (L2)

(3) Use two blocks, one on each side of the feet, to support your hands. (L3)

(4) With the thighs against a wall. (L3)

(5) Keep a block between the thighs. (L2)

(6) Pressing thighs, calves, and feet together. (L3)

(7) Cross arms behind you and take hold of opposite ankles. (L3)

## SUPINE POSES

### WIND-RELIEF POSE/KNEE-TO-CHEST POSE (*APANASANA/PAVANMUKTASANA*) (L2)

*Benefits*: Strengthens the arms, shoulders, back, legs, and hips; stretches the chest, obliques, and glutes. Alleviates back pain. Firms abdominal muscles, increases flexibility around the hips. Improves blood circulation (great for varicose veins). Massages abdominal area, relieves painful trapped gas in the intestines, improves constipation.

With one leg: Lie on your back with legs stretched out together. Inhale slowly, bend the right knee and bring it toward the chest. Hold the posture 30 seconds to a minute while breathing. Exhale and release the leg. Repeat twice more, then switch sides.

With both legs: Lie on your back with legs together. Bend both knees and, exhaling, bring them to the chest. Hold onto the knees with hands clasped around them and hug them to the chest.

Inhale deeply. Extend the crown and, exhaling, bring navel down and raise the head slowly up and in between the knees. On an inhale, slowly lower the head. Continue hugging the knees and breathing deeply. On an exhale, release the legs down, straighten the legs onto the floor, and take a long stretch with arms reaching upward and away from the feet.

### RECLINED SPINAL TWIST (*SUPTA MATSYENDRASANA*) (L2)

*Benefits*: Stretches the chest, glutes, obliques, and back muscles. Realigns and lengthens the spine, hydrates the spinal disks, improves constipation.

Lie down on your back. Stretch out the arms perpendicular to the body at shoulder height. Bend the knees, keeping them together. With thighs perpendicular to the ground, slowly exhale while lowering the knees together to the right. Turn your head to the left. Breathe. Make sure arms don't lift off the mat. With an inhale, bring the legs back to the center. Exhale, let the knees drop to the left until they touch the floor. Inhale, bring the knees up to the center. Exhale, relax the legs. Switch sides.

VARIATIONS:

(1) Bring knees higher and the opposite hand can hold the knee. (L2)

(2) Put right arm on the floor, palm down, and on an exhale bring the right bent leg to the left side. The right hip should be stacked on top of the left hip. Hold down the knee gently with the left hand. Right arm should be perpendicular to the body on the ground. If it is comfortable, turn your head to the right to gaze at your hand. Release and switch sides. (L2)

### STRAIGHT-LEG RAISE (*EKA PADA UTTANA PADASANA*) (L1)

*Benefits*: Tones and strengthens the lower back, abdominal, calf, thigh, hamstring, and gluteus muscles; improves flexibility; tones the muscles and ligaments of the uterus and pelvic muscles. Improves digestion; good for constipation.

⚠ For those with potential lower back problems, raise one leg at a time.

Lie on back with straight legs, arms to the side, palms down. On an inhale, slowly bring the right leg up to 90 degrees. Hold for 30 seconds. Breathe. Exhale and bring the leg down.

Repeat on the same side a few times, then switch sides.

Lie on back with straight legs. Bend the left leg. On an inhale, slowly bring the right leg straight up as if to hold the ceiling on your foot. Hold it and breath slowly and deeply. On an exhale, release the leg slowly down. Switch sides. (L2)

Alternatively, exhale as you raise your head and upper back off the ground and reach out with the hands around the straight leg. Hold on to the back of the knee and breathe deeply and slowly. Exhale and release the leg. Switch sides. (L2)

VARIATIONS:

(1) Use a strap or belt around the sole of the foot to hoist the leg gently toward you. (L1)

(2) Lying on the floor, raise both legs at the same time. Watch that lower back remains on the ground. You can ground your hands, palms down, under the buttocks. (L3)

(3) Use a small cushion or rolled-up towel under the small of the back. (L1)

### SIDE-RECLINING VISHNU COUCH POSE (*ANANTASANA*) (L2)

*Benefits*: Stretches the hamstrings, inner thighs, and calves; tones the abdominal muscles; improves balance; increases blood circulation; improves digestion.

Lie on your back. Roll onto your left side. Stretch your left arm over your head. Bend your left elbow and cradle your head in your hand. Stabilize yourself with the right hand. Slowly rotate and lift your right leg so that the toes point to the ceiling. Hold the pose for 30 to 60 seconds. Breathe normally. Slowly release and come back on your back. Repeat the posture on the other side.

VARIATION:

(1) Hold on to the big toe of the extended foot with the hand. (L2)

## INVERSIONS

### PLOW POSE (*HALASANA*) (L3)

*Benefits*: Stretches and tones almost all the muscle groups of the body. Rejuvenating, as circulation increases around the face. Stimulates the thyroid gland, pancreas, liver, kidneys, and reproductive glands. Reduces menopausal symptoms, improves digestion, helps insomnia. Calms the nervous system.

⚠ This pose is advanced and can lead to cervical trauma. If you are advanced enough, please do this posture slowly and wisely. Keep the head straight and the neck long.

Lie on your back with your buttocks on a bolster, arms by your sides, palms facing down. Inhale and lift the legs from the floor without bending them. Your abs are strong enough to do this. Lift the buttocks off the floor with the arms and hands pushing down on the floor. Exhaling, slowly bring the legs up and over your head, keeping them extended straight, toes touching the ground if possible. Hold the posture 30–60 seconds. On an exhale, slowly bring the legs back one vertebra at a time. Give yourself some time to recuperate.

VARIATIONS:
(1) If you find it difficult at the beginning, you can lie in front of a wall, putting your feet on the wall to give yourself some propulsion. (L2)
(2) Make a small platform with some folded bolsters, blankets, or towels for extra comfort. (L2)
(3) You can place your hands on your love handles to control the movement. (L2)
(4) Bend the knees and use a slight rocking motion. (L2)
(5) Put some blocks behind the head where the feet land.

### HEADSTAND (*SHIRSHASANA*) (L3)

*Benefits*: Strengthens the core and shoulders. Regulates the endocrine system; increases blood flow to the brain, scalp, and facial tissues. Improves digestion. Aids concentration, memory, and anxiety.

⚠ This pose is advanced and can lead to cervical trauma. If you are advanced enough, do this posture slowly and wisely.

Although headstands are considered the most difficult posture, using a special padded stool can make them child's play. At first, have someone help you and put the stool next to a wall for support. Have a non-slip mat underneath for maximum safety.

Stand in front of the stool with shins against the front. Bend down, holding the front of the stool with both hands. Lower the crown of your head into the hole. Slowly put the weight of your shoulders onto the padded cushions as if you were going to dive into the space below. Walk your feet close to the front of the stool. Keep your thighs close to your belly and chest to begin. Experiment with slowly lifting one foot off the floor. Enjoy learning a new way to balance. If you feel confident enough, lift the other foot off the floor. Slowly start unfolding your legs till they are straight above you. Breathe.

VARIATIONS:

(1) With the help of someone, on a pile of blankets, against a wall. Be very careful with the neck when doing handstands, as a lot of weight is put on the fragile cervical disks. (L3)

(2) Once the feet are up, you can confidently start opening the feet apart, bending one leg.

## RESTORATIVE POSES

### HALF-INVERTED POSE, LEGS UP A WALL (*VIPARITA KARANI*) (L1)

*Benefits*: Stretches the hamstrings and lower back; relieves lower back pain. Good for low blood pressure and lymphatic drainage. Helps beat insomnia, improves digestion, relaxing and soothing.

⚠ Avoid it if you have high blood pressure!

You can start a session with this posture when you are feeling drained. Fold a blanket a few inches away from the wall. Lie on your back next to the wall with the buttocks inside the space. The lower back is supported on the blanket. Swing your legs up so that your buttocks are against the wall and legs are perpendicular to the mat. Breathe deeply and mindfully. To get out of this position, exhale, bring the knees to the chest and roll to the side. Press with the hands into easy pose.

VARIATION:

(1) Open legs into a wide V shape.

(2) Keep knees bent if it is difficult to straighten the legs.

(3) Use the back of a chair to rest your ankles to create a lower angle between the body and legs.

### WIDE-KNEE CHILD'S POSE (*UTTHITA BALASANA*) (L1)

*Benefits*: Stretches the spine, hips, thighs, and calves; helps relieve back and neck pain; rejuvenates the pelvic region; relieves stress and fatigue, increases circulation; fights insomnia.

This position is more suitable for women with sensitive breasts: Sitting on your heels, slowly move to all fours. Exhale, open your knees to touch the outside of your mat. Toes touch. Bring the chest to the mat. Keep space between your ears and shoulders. Try to bring the hips toward the heels and your belly between your thighs. The arms stretch forward or remain along the body. Jaw is relaxed. Forehead on the ground. To come out of the position, inhale, lift up, and bring the knees together.

### CHILD'S POSE (*BALASANA*) (L1)

*Benefits*: Strengthens the spine and abdominal region and ankles; relieves neck, back, and hip pain; helps constipation; restorative and calming, treats anxiety and insomnia.

Sitting on your heels, slowly move to all fours, exhale, and lower the hips to the heels.

Exhaling, bring your torso forward, over the thighs. Place your forehead on the ground. Bring your arms next to your body, palms up, and let their weight open the shoulders. Hold the pose for a minute as you breathe deeply. Inhale and raise the torso and straighten the spine.

VARIATION:

(1) Arms in front in prayer (*Namaste*) mudra. (L1)

(2) Forehead on a block or cheek on a blanket. (L1)

(3) With one arm under the body, perpendicular to the torso. (L2)

### REVERSE CORPSE POSE (*ADVASANA*) (L1)

*Benefits*: Relieves back and neck pain. Good for slipped discs. Deeply relaxing. Good to counteract fatigue. Improves digestion. Decreases anxiety and stress.

Lie on stomach with arms stretched by body, legs parallel and slightly apart. Rest the forehead on the mat or turn the head to place one cheek on the mat. Breathe consciously.

VARIATIONS:

(1) Place hand under the forehead to act as a cushion.

(2) Stretch arms ahead to allow the spine to stretch.

### CORPSE POSE (*SHAVASANA*) (L1)

*Benefits*: Relaxation and rejuvenation, reduces insomnia, lowers blood pressure, aids the digestion and headaches, reduces anxiety.

It is a good idea to end your daily practice with this pose, to allow the mind and body to recuperate. Lie down on your back on your mat. Your body is straight and symmetrical.

Arms are along the body, palms facing up, fingers like unfurling leaves. Legs are hip-distance apart with the feet slightly open. Eyes are closed. The jaw, teeth, and tongue are relaxed, the mouth is closed. Turn your awareness inside and focus on the heart center with each breath.

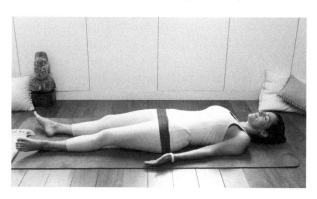

VARIATIONS:

(1) Eye pillow on the eyes for deep relaxation. (L1)

(2) Blanket to cover oneself, as the body temperature will drop. (L1)

(3) Bolster under the knees. (L1)

(4) Cushion under the neck. (L1)

### Coming Out of Corpse Pose

Arms open and stretched over the head, palms facing upward. Rotate wrists. Stretch the feet forward and flex them. Make small rotating movements with the ankles. Rub soles of feet and palms of the hands together to bring some energy and heat back. Cover the eyes with the cushions of the palms. Massage the eye sockets and temples. Open your eyes. Roll onto one side and push yourself up with one hand. Once you are standing, you may stamp your feet lightly and stretch a little in different directions to reorient and feel grounded to your external environment.

# Shopping List

+ Meditation bench (preferably with curved feet)
+ Slip-proof gym/yoga mat (I personally love those with markings that help you to align)
+ Soft (washable) blanket
+ Eye mask or bean bag for eyes (if you find one stuffed with lavender, it is a pure delight)
+ Essential oils (clary sage)
+ Meditation cushions (they come in all shapes and sizes, try them out before buying; I personally love my light bean bag cushion that can double as a pillow for relaxation and is light enough for traveling)
+ Padded stool for headstands (only if you are advanced enough to safely do the pose)
+ Fan
+ Yoga blocks
+ Bolster
+ Crayons or felt-tips
+ Coconut oil


Additional, but not essential, paraphernalia:
+ Incense sticks
+ Candles

# References

Amodeo, John. *Dancing with Fire: A Mindful Way to Loving Relationships.* Wheaton, IL: Quest Books, 2013.

Barks, Coleman, trans. *The Essential Rumi.* London: Penguin, 1995.

———, trans. *Rumi: The Book of Love: Poems of Ecstasy and Longing.* New York: Harper Collins, 2003.

Bénézet, C. *Kundalini & Me: Sur le chemin de la transformation avec le yoga.* Paris: Marabout, 2020.

Berkson, D. Lindsey. *Safe Hormones, Smart Women.* Scotts Valley, CA: CreateSpace Independent Publishing Platform, 2010.

Brach, Tara. *True Refuge: Finding Peace and Freedom in Your Own Awakened Heart.* New York: Bantam Books, 2012.

Burnap, George Washington. *The Sphere and Duties of Woman: A Course of Lectures.* Buffalo, NY: Zenger Publishing Co., 1975.

Camus, Albert. *Lyrical and Critical Essays.* Edited by Philip Thody. Translated by Ellen Conroy Kennedy. New York: Vintage Books, 1968.

Cantoni, Louis J. "Walt Whitman, Secular Mystic." *The Personalist* 36.4 (1955): 379–84.

Carmody, J., S. Crawford, E. Salmoirago-Blotcher, K. Leung, L. Churchill, and N. Olendzki. "Mindfulness Training for Coping with Hot Flashes: Results of a Randomized Trial." *Menopause* 18.6 (2011): 611–20. doi: 10.1097/gme.0b013e318204a05c.

Erdmuth Lotze-Kola, Dorothea. *Inspirations for Today: A Daily Devotional.* Bloomington, IN: iUniverse, 2018. (Source of E. E. Cummings quote for August 29.)

Evenson, R., and R. Simon. "Clarifying the Relationship between Parenthood and Depression." *Journal of Health and Social Behavior* 46.4 (2005): 341–58.

Flaubert, Gustave. *Madame Bovary.* New York: Bantam Classics, 1981.

García, Héctor, and Francesc Miralles. *Ikigai: The Japanese Secret to a Long and Happy Life.* New York: Penguin, 2017.

Golle, J., F. W. Mast, and J. S. Lobmaier. "Something to Smile About: The Interrelationship between Attractiveness and Emotional Expression." *Cognition & Emotion* 28.2 (2014): 298–310.

Gunaratana, Bhante. *Mindfulness in Plain English.* Somerville, MA: Wisdom Publications, 2015 [1995].

Helwig, N., N. E. Sohre, M. R. Ruprecht, S. J. Guy, and S. Lyford-Pike. "Dynamic Properties of Successful Smiles." *PloS ONE* 12.6 (2017): e0179708. https://doi.org/10.1371/journal.pone.0179708.

*Jing Si Aphorisms.* https://www.tzuchi.org.tw/en/index.php?option=com_content&view=article &id=1110%3Ajing-si-aphorisms-englishfrancaisdeutsch-italiano&catid=91%3Ajing-si-publi

cation-&Itemid=154&lang=en. The Tzu Chi Cultural Publishing Co. Posted June 12, 2013. Accessed December 3, 2020.

Kabat-Zinn, Jon. *Full Catastrophe Living: Using the Wisdom of Your Body and Mind to Face Stress, Pain, and Illness*. Revised and updated edition. New York: Bantam Books, 2013 [1990].

———. *Wherever You Go, There You Are: Mindfulness Meditation in Everyday Life*. New York: Hachette Books, 2009 [1994].

Kaminoff, Leslie, and Amy Matthews. *Yoga Anatomy*. Leeds: Human Kinetics, 2012.

Kaur, R. *The Sun and Her Flowers*. New York: Simon & Schuster, 2017.

Kelsang Nyema, Gen. "Happiness Is All in Your Mind." June 2014. https://www.youtube.com/watch?v=xnLoToJVQH4.

Komjathy, L. *Taming the Wild Horse: An Annotated Translation and Study of the Daoist Horse Taming Pictures*. New York: Columbia University Press, 2017.

Kostov, Nayden. "Find the Mistake Quizz." 2017. https://www.raiseyourbrain.com/find-mistake-quiz/.

Kraft, T. L., and S. D. Pressman. "Grin and Bear It: The Influence of Manipulated Facial Expression on the Stress Response." *Psychological Science* 23.11 (2012): 1372–78.

Kristeller, J. L., R. Q. Wolever, and V. Sheets. "Mindfulness-Based Eating Awareness Training (MB-EAT) for Binge Eating: A Randomized Clinical Trial." *Mindfulness* 5.3: 282–97.

Kyōkai, Bukkyō Dendō. *The Teachings of Buddha*. New York: Sterling Publishers Pvt. Ltd., 2005.

Lawson, JonArno, and Sydney Smith. *Sidewalk Flowers*. Berkeley, CA: Groundwood Books, 2015.

Levinson, Sam. *In One Era and Out the Other*. New York: Simon & Schuster, 1929.

Lilly, Sue. *A Complete Guide to Understanding and Practising Yoga*. London: Caxton Publishing Group, 2001.

Lutkehaus, N. *Margaret Mead: The Making of an American Icon*. Princeton, NJ: Princeton University Press, 2018.

Morello, Tai. *The Yoga Beginner's Bible: Top 63 Illustrated Poses for Weight Loss, Stress Relief and Inner Peace*. 3d ed. N.p, 2015.

Oh, Byeongsang, Kyung Ju Lee, Chris Zaslawski, Albert Yeung, David Rosenthal, Linda Larkey, and Michael Back. "Health and Well-Being Benefits of Spending Time in Forests: Systematic Review." *Environmental Health and Preventive Medicine* 22.1 (2017): 71. doi: DOI: 10.1186/s12199-017-0677-9.

Park, S., and K. Han. "Blood Pressure Response to Meditation and Yoga: A Systematic Review and Meta-Analysis." *The Journal of Alternative and Complementary Medicine* 23.9 (2017): 685–95.

Roudeau, Cécile. "'Like Islands in the Sea': Intermingled Consciousness and the Politics of the Self in Sarah Orne Jewett's Late Stories." *William James Studies* 13.2 (2017): 190–216.

Schucman, H., and W. N. Thetford. *A Course in Miracles: Combined Volume*. Mill Valley, CA: Foundation for Inner Peace, 1996.

Segal, Z., J. Teasdale, and M. Williams. "Mindfulness-Based Cognitive Therapy: Theoretical Rationale and Empirical Status." In *Mindfulness and Acceptance: Expanding the Cognitive-Behavioral Tradition*, edited by S. C. Hayes, V. M. Follette, and M. M. Linehan, 45–65. New York: Guilford Press, 2004.

Siegel, J., F. Angulo, R. Detels, J. Wesch, and A. Mullen. "AIDS Diagnosis and Depression in the Multicenter AIDS Cohort Study: The Ameliorating Impact of Pet Ownership." *Aids Care* 11.2 (1999): 157–70.

Sri Chinmoy. *Sound Becomes, Silence Is*. London: Agni Press, 1975.

Stahl, Bob, and Elisha Goldstein. *A Mindfulness-Based Stress Reduction Workbook*. Oakland, CA: New Harbinger Publications, 2010.

Tagore, Rabindranath. *The Home and the World*. London: Macmillan, 1919.

Teasdale, John, Mark Williams, and Zindel Segal. *The Mindful Way Workbook: An 8-Week Program to Free Yourself from Depression and Emotional Distress*. New York: Guilford Press, 2014.

Thich Nhat Hanh. *How to Eat*. San Francisco: Parallax Press, 2014.

———. *The Miracle of Mindfulness: An Introduction to Mindfulness*. Boston: Beacon Press, 1996.

———. *The Miracle of Mindfulness: A Manual on Meditation*. Boston: Beacon Press, 1987.

Tolle, Eckhard. *The Power of Now*. London: Hodder and Stoughton, 2011.

Travers, J. *A Puzzle-Mine: Puzzles Collected from the Works of the Late Henry Ernest Dudeney*. Nashville: Thomas Nelson and Sons, 1951.

Vira, S., B. Diebo, M. Spiegel, et al. "Is There a Gender-Specific Full-Body Saggital Profile for Different Spinopelvic Relationships? A Study on Propensity-Matched Cohort." *Spine Deformity* 4.2 (2016): 104–11.

Wallace, B. Alan. *Minding Closely: The Four Applications of Mindfulness*. Ithaca, NY: Snow Lion Publications, 2011.

Whitman, W. "A Song for Occupations." [1881–82] The Walt Whitman Archive. Edited by Matt Cohen, Ed Folsom, and Kenneth M. Price. Published by the Center for Digital Research in the Humanities at the University of Nebraska-Lincoln. https://whitmanarchive.org/published/LG/1881/poems/94.

Winnicott, Donald Woods. *Winnicott on the Child*. Boston: Da Capo Lifelong Books, 2009.

# About the Author

FRANCESCA DUPRAZ-BROSSARD is a state-registered cognitive-behavioral psychotherapist who works in private practice in Geneva, Switzerland. She works with couples and individuals. She is proficient in the use of hypnosis, mindfulness, schema therapy, and yoga, which she weaves together in her unique therapeutic approach. She is a member of the British Psychological Society (BPS), Swiss Society of Psychologists (FSP), Swiss Institute of Hypnosis (IRHyS), Swiss Society of Clinical Hypnosis (SHyPS), Swiss Association of Complementary Medicine (ASCA), Swiss Association of Cognitive Psychotherapy (ASPCo), Swiss Society of Sexology (SSS), International Society of Schema Therapy (ISST), L'Institut Sexocorporel International (ISI), and European Society of Sexual Medicine (ESSM).

Of British origin, with a Spanish mother and French paternal grandparents, Dupraz-Brossard grew up in London. She has lived in Spain, Egypt, Cyprus, and Saudi Arabia. She is a mother of three grown daughters and a stepmother to two. She lives between the countryside of Geneva and the Bernese mountains, where she enjoys nature and walking with her two dogs.

# What to Read Next
# from Wisdom Publications

**The Grace in Aging**
*Awaken as You Grow Older*
Kathleen Dowling Singh

"Don't grow old without it."
—Rachel Naomi Remen, MD, author of *Kitchen Table Wisdom*

**Aging for Beginners**
Ezra Bayda

Winner of the *Spirituality & Practice* Best Book Award in 2019

**Mindfulness Yoga**
*The Awakened Union of Breath, Body, and Mind*
Frank Jude Boccio

Editor's Choice
—*Yoga Journal*

**The Hidden Lamp**
*Stories from Twenty-Five Centuries of Awakened Women*
Edited by Zenshin Florence Caplow and Reigetsu Susan Moon
Foreword by Norman Fischer

"An amazing collection. This book gives the wonderful feel of the sincerity, the great range, and the nobility of the spiritual work that women are doing and have been doing, unacknowledged, for a very long time. An essential and delightful book."
—John Tarrant, author of *The Light Inside the Dark: Zen, Soul, and the Spiritual Life*

# About Wisdom Publications

Wisdom Publications is the leading publisher of classic and contemporary Buddhist books and practical works on mindfulness. To learn more about us or to explore our other books, please visit our website at wisdomexperience.org or contact us at the address below.

Wisdom Publications
199 Elm Street
Somerville, MA 02144 USA

We are a 501(c)(3) organization, and donations in support of our mission are tax deductible.

Wisdom Publications is affiliated with the Foundation for the Preservation of the Mahayana Tradition (FPMT).